SPEAK EASY

SPEAK EASY

A Field Guide to Love, Longing and Intimacy

SEEMA ANAND

with inputs from
Dr Anvita Madan-Bahel

BLOOMSBURY
NEW DELHI • LONDON • OXFORD • NEW YORK • SYDNEY

BLOOMSBURY INDIA
Bloomsbury Publishing India Pvt. Ltd
Second Floor, LSC Building No. 4, DDA Complex,
Pocket C – 6 & 7, Vasant Kunj,
New Delhi 110070

BLOOMSBURY, BLOOMSBURY INDIA and the Diana logo are
trademarks of Bloomsbury Publishing Plc

First published in India 2025

Copyright © Seema Anand, 2025
Copyright for expert advice pieces vests with respective contributors

Seema Anand has asserted her right under the
Indian Copyright Act to be identified as the Author of this work

This book is not a substitute for medical attention, treatment, examination, advice, treatment of existing conditions or diagnosis. It is not intended to provide a clinical diagnosis nor take the place of medical advice from a fully qualified medical practitioner. Consult your healthcare service provider before following any health advice given in this book.

This book contains references to sensitive subjects including self-harm, suicide and sexual assault. These references are included solely for literary and educational purposes and are not intended to endorse, encourage or trivialise such conduct. Readers are strongly advised to exercise discretion, particularly if such themes may cause distress. The author and publisher disclaim responsibility for any adverse emotional or psychological impact arising from engagement with these passages. Readers who are affected are encouraged to seek professional support or contact appropriate helplines in their jurisdiction

All rights reserved. No part of this publication may be: i) reproduced or transmitted in any form, electronic or mechanical, including photocopying, recording or by means of any information storage or retrieval system without prior permission in writing from the publishers; or ii) used or reproduced in any way for the training, development or operation of artificial intelligence (AI) technologies, including generative AI technologies. The rights holders expressly reserve this publication from the text and data mining exception as per Article 4(3) of the Digital Single Market Directive (EU) 2019/790

ISBN: HB: 978-93-61319-33-4; eBook: 978-93-61310-98-0
2 4 6 8 10 9 7 5 3 1

Printed and bound in India by Thomson Press India Ltd.

To find out more about our authors and books, visit
www.bloomsbury.com and sign up for our newsletters

For my children
Monica, Nikhil, Varun, Tarini and Naia
I face the backlash, the judgement and the trolls
so I can clear the path for a better world for you

Contents

Preface   xi

Part 1   Relationship Structures

1. I feel his desire for adventure is stronger than his interest in monogamy   5
2. Are these emotions normal? I don't even know what I want from this   10
3. He says it is not cheating because he has told me about it   14
4. The spark in our sex life has faded   19
5. I tell myself maybe this time it will feel different   24
6. When I confronted him, he broke down and began to justify his actions   28
7. We started our relationship knowing that we can't meet for at least a year   31
8. More than participating, it was watching them that started exciting me   35
9. How the man/woman can de-stress and disconnect mentally from work   38
10. I regret bringing it up, but I was being honest and trusting   41
11. I told him to block her and don't engage, she's only 17   44
12. Dating as a single parent   48

Part 2   Different Minds

13. While we share intimacy in other ways, I cannot handle penetration   58

14. We were good in the first two years, but then I lost interest — 63
15. I feel we are mismatched and I may have married the wrong person — 66
16. I feel stuck in conservative ideas when it comes to myself — 70
17. Is there a way to reduce my libido or increase hers? — 73
18. Is something wrong with me – am I bad at sex? — 77
19. My boyfriend has a problem with my previous relationship — 81
20. Because of my inexperience I don't know how good it can actually feel — 84
21. I feel like shaking her to come to her senses and use science/logic — 88
22. When it comes to sex, he just watches porn and masturbates as it is easier and less work — 91
23. I like porn and sometimes I watch just to fill the gap in the day — 94
24. We have just moved in together and suddenly he doesn't want sex — 98
25. Stuck at the initial stage, I cannot start even though it's my wife — 101

Part 3 Navigating Queerness

26. Now my partner is being forced by his family to marry a girl, and he has agreed — 109
27. I knew he liked to cross-dress, and at first I was OK with it — 112
28. In my 30s, I began feeling intensely aroused by transwomen — 116
29. He wants to end it as he wants to have a wife who can give him kids — 120
30. I get confused and lonely and miss the intimacy I had with my late wife — 123

Part 4 Pain During Sex

31. Why do some positions cause pain? 131
32. Urinary tract infections 135
33. Discharges and pain during sex 138
34. Sexually transmitted diseases 141
35. Pelvic inflammatory disease 144
36. Vaginismus 146
37. Vulvodynia 150

Part 5 Bodily Functions

38. My wife is very loud, especially during climax 157
39. Should I lighten it with bleaching or cosmetic surgery? 160
40. My husband laughs when I pass wind but this is not my idea of sexy 163
41. Why do I find the idea of sex better than the actual sex? 168
42. I have unfortunately been through female genital mutilation 172
43. Now I can't orgasm any other way 175
44. Does the vulva come out with masturbation? 178
45. Is the hymen supposed to tear, does it actually tear? 181
46. Does the vagina become loose with sex? 185
47. How can I prepare emotionally for first-time sex? 189
48. Contraception 193
49. I've never experienced orgasm in our relationship 197
50. What does an orgasm feel like? 200
51. Sex in the 50s for menopausal women 204
52. A colorectal surgeon's advice on anal sex 207
53. Sensations and safe practices during anal play 211
54. BDSM to heal trauma and rebalance emotions 215
55. A practical guide to squirting 219
56. I have weak erection and only last a few seconds 222
57. Does size matter? 226

Part 6 Conflict Resolution

58. Each time I try to end it my partner threatens suicide — 235
59. How can a woman who has experienced sexual abuse reconnect with her body — 238
60. Non-consensual intimate videos — 242
61. I found out he was exchanging nudes with a woman — 246
62. Whenever I think of sex or masturbate, my ex comes into my head — 249
63. I usually get very bad dreams which includes sex — 253

Acknowledgements — 255
Resource List — 257
About the Author — 259

Preface

When I first began speaking publicly about pleasure, its importance – but also the guilt, stigma and stereotypes that surround it – I discovered something I had not anticipated: that simply by breaking the silence, you become a place of refuge, you become that someone who might hold an answer in a world where questions about sex are usually met with shame or silence.

Back then, the messages were almost always from men, blunt, single-dimensional and circling around the same themes – 'how do I last longer', 'why can't I get an erection', 'how do I increase my size' – real concerns in their own way but reflecting the limited vocabulary people had to ask for help and information.

Over time, as I have continued to speak on the subject the shift has been striking, with questions now coming equally from across the gender spectrum and becoming far more nuanced, moving beyond performance into deeper concerns like how to return to desire after trauma or why desire can vanish in the safety of a stable relationship instead of growing or even how to speak to a partner about a fantasy without being judged.

What this revealed to me was that despite societal repression people want to be able to understand and explore their desires, they need information and guidance but had never been given permission to ask, and hence anyone speaking on the subject automatically becomes the default space for sex education. It's like opening the floodgates.

In my case, there was an added layer. Because of my background in the study of the *Kama Sutra* and the erotic texts of ancient India, almost every message I received included the question 'what does the *Kama Sutra* say about this', which made me realise that more than simply a question, this was also a search for validation, that their problem had an answer rooted in wisdom older than themselves. In a world that often tells us that sexual desire is 'against our culture' or a form of 'Western corruption', people were looking for reassurance that their needs were also recognised in their own traditions.

What also quickly became clear was that these questions could not be answered in 60-second reels. A meaningful answer requires context, explanation and balanced information. Sexuality is not just about technique, it is about conditioning, culture, history, psychology and the hidden narratives we carry within ourselves. And a couple of lines on social media cannot untangle years of shame, silence or misinformation.

This book comes out of that intersection. Under the expert guidance of psychosexual and relational therapist Dr Anvita Madan-Bahel and all our wonderful experts, and drawing on my own studies and lived experience – because at this age experience itself becomes a form of knowledge, adding a depth no textbook can capture – *Speak Easy* offers careful, thoughtful answers grounded in cultural and emotional contexts to questions that are both universal and as old as time.

While many chapters are written in my voice, others are drawn from the expertise of specialists – medical guidance comes directly from doctors, the chapter on female genital mutilation is written by someone who has lived through it, and the one on 'squirting' is contributed by an expert in the field.

Each chapter takes a real question and responds to it in depth, with honesty and clarity, because these are not trivial doubts, they affect people's confidence, their marriages and their ability to feel safe in their own bodies.

When people write in, what they are really seeking is someone to help them through not just the confusion and fear but also the loneliness of carrying a doubt or a question with no one to trust. This book is our attempt to provide accurate information, thoughtful analysis and practical guidance to anyone who has ever felt silenced.

Seema Anand

Part 1

Relationship Structures

When I moved from the field of comprehensive sexuality education to training as a psychosexual therapist, my biggest learning was the sheer breadth of sexual diversity among people. Interest in different sexual activities was far more common than I could ever have imagined. During training, one of our colleagues had joked about feeling like 'a virgin in a whorehouse' – a sentiment I could well relate to. Even something as simple as a group visit to an erotica shop had highlighted just how vast the world of erotica toys and materials was, and how limited our own knowledge and exposure to it.

Through this course I was exposed to conversations about a wide range of sexual interests – from threesomes and fetishes to kink, swinging, cross-dressing and chemsex parties. What struck me most was that, despite the repression drilled into us, so many people not only desired these experiences but were already practising them. With my clients, and later with listeners of the podcast I co-host with Seema, I found more and more people willing to open up about everything from foot fetishes and cuckoldry to swinging, fantasies about neighbours and even incest because they had finally found a safe space in which to share and seek reliable information.

There are no straightforward boxes for sexual diversity, it is infinite and constantly revealing new forms of expression. Yet for most people these desires remain steeped in fear and shame, with one constant refrain, that 'friends and family must never know'. Many worry that liking something unusual means there is something wrong with them, that it makes them abnormal or that they will never find a partner who may accept and share their interests. And so they live with the weight of secrecy, unable to ever express themselves fully.

When advising people, I found fantasies easier to work with. I often described them as tools to help stimulate arousal. They create completely imaginary worlds, such as being aroused at the thought of having sex on a parachute or while swimming in the ocean. Because they exist only in the mind, fantasies can be anything we imagine. Whether kept private or shared with a partner to enhance arousal, they were generally easier for people to accept.

Fetishes, however, raised more complicated questions. Many people knew what excited them but worried about being seen as 'weird' or 'abnormal'. Some were relieved to discover how many other people had the same fetish, while others had researched obsessively online and often overwhelmed themselves with information. But in the end, the real challenge was not what they knew about it but how to communicate it to their partner, and whether it would be accepted.

This complexity often played out in relationships.

Some people, unsure about how to communicate their desires, secretly obsessed over their fetish until it disrupted their sex lives. Others managed to share openly, with partners agreeing to try it as well, but this often led to further complications. In many cases, people said yes because they feared that a no would incite their partners to leave them or cheat on them. Some worried about what would happen if they said yes but didn't end up enjoying it. Due to our patchy understanding of the concept of consent, many felt that once they had agreed, they were committed forever, that there was no room to say no the next time. And so, many partners agreed reluctantly, fearing rejection.

For some, taking the risk of trying something new paid off, as they discovered new sources of pleasure. In other cases, when the activity was not enjoyable, partners often stayed silent out of fear that speaking up might threaten the relationship, and over time that silence created tension within the relationship. And in many cases, we found that the partner who wanted their own fetish explored, although comfortable asking for the experiment, found they couldn't handle it when the roles were reversed, leading to jealousy and conflict in the relationship.

When faced with something outside your 'norm', my advice is always to hear out your partner before you make any decisions.

Sexual desires and fetishes are normal, but pleasure is also very individual, so it is essential for you to consider whether engaging in them will be genuinely arousing for you. If you dislike the idea but do it only to please your partner, you are likely to resent the experience, and that resentment can damage the relationship. Engage only if you are willing to give it a fair chance.

It is completely acceptable to say, 'I am open to trying this, but I cannot promise I will enjoy it.' This keeps the option of refusal open if the experience is uncomfortable. Some people feel they have no choice and end up stuck in activities that make them uneasy. Others may be comfortable experimenting up to a certain point but not beyond it, or they may be fine when it is done on their terms but not when their partner does the same – and all of this will impact your relationship.

These complications show why it is so important to reflect carefully on your own boundaries. Never engage in activities under pressure or solely to satisfy your partner. Remember, consent is not just essential, it needs to be freely given and must be revocable at all times.

Healthy exploration depends on awareness, reflection, open communication, clear boundaries and, above all, consent. Whether or not you choose to explore your desires, it is important that you acknowledge them to yourself. Sexual diversity is endless, and as long as what you are doing is safe, consensual and not harming anyone, if it brings you pleasure, no one has the right to judge your choices.

Dr Anvita Madan-Bahel

My husband and I are very good and compatible in bed. Over time, we have become emotionally closer, and open about our fantasies. For him, this included wanting to see me having sex with another guy. Although I was not comfortable with the idea, I decided to do it for him. We went to another country and there we called a paid 'bull' and I had sex with him while my husband watched. Later, my husband told me he kissed another woman but could not perform sexually. He flirts with his colleague but insists it is harmless, I worry it will go further. They recently went to a pub together, and she asked him to take her to a hotel. He declined and called me instead, but it still hurts.

He now wants a threesome. While I sometimes get excited thinking about it, deep down I know I do not want to share him. I have told him this, and though he promises not to sleep with anyone else, I feel his desire for adventure is stronger than his interest in monogamy. I keep thinking, if he has sex with someone else and tells me, is it still cheating? Or did I already cross that line when I went through with his fantasy, even though I did not really want to? I am confused, uncomfortable, and scared.

Traditionally, 'cuckold' was a humiliating label for a man whose wife had cheated, a nagging, complaining husband who had driven his wife into the arms of another with his bad behaviour.

Today, the term has evolved within kink and BDSM, where consensual cuckolding is a form of shared arousal rooted in self-subversion and masochism. But while in secure relationships it can be an intensely arousing, guilt-free fetish, for the ordinary person who has watched/understood it from the half context of porn, it is being increasingly misused, with consent being replaced by coercion and many men pressuring their partners into it under the guise of emotional depth or adventure.

I notice from your message that your greatest guilt (and obstacle) to voicing your feelings is the fact that you 'enjoyed' the act even though you were uncomfortable – let's be clear: your enjoyment of the act does not mean you truly wanted it. What people don't talk about enough is the fact that our bodies respond to stimulation even when we don't emotionally want it. It's called arousal non-concordance, a term in psychology that explains how the body can react to sexual stimuli even when the mind doesn't consent.

There is an interesting story in our Puranas of the sage Gautam cursing his wife Ahalya for something that was clearly not her fault. Indra, the king of gods, lusting after Ahalya but having been turned down consistently by her, disguises himself as her husband to seduce her. Initially, she has no idea that it is not her husband. Somewhere along the lovemaking, realisation dawns upon her, but, we are told, she is too far into her pleasure to be able to stop.

And it is for this feeling of 'pleasure' that her husband puts a curse on her. Her body, according to him, betrayed her inner desires, proving her adulterous intentions, making her worthy of the curse.

In fact, becoming wet during uncomfortable experiences, even when those stimuli are 'disgusting or appalling or horrifying', just means that the sexually relevant signals in your brain are being cued. A genital response is not desire or pleasure, it is simply sexually relevant. As Emily Nagoski says, 'If my mouth waters when I bite into a wormy apple, does anybody say to me, "You said no, but your body said yes?"'* The body has its own reactions to the pleasure and arousal you feel during good sex (you mentioned you had paid for a 'bull', this is his profession, he understands how

---

* Julie Balsiger, 'WTF Is Unwanted Arousal? Consent 101', *Elephant Journal*, 16 May 2020. In the article, Balsiger quotes Emily Nagoski.

to bring you to complete arousal). So the first thing is to stop beating yourself up.

Marriage is a contract with some unwritten rules and one of the most basic ones is an expectation of monogamy. You did not ask for a mutual change of terms, you did not break the contract – your husband changed that part of the contract for his needs. It was his idea from the start. *He* asked for you to have sex with another man for *his* arousal and pleasure experiments. And yes, he felt it would be for your mutual arousal; but even after you declined a few times and told him you didn't want to do it, he still insisted you try it because it was primarily for his pleasure.

You have every right to tell him that this is not something you want to do, that far from being of interest, it makes you deeply unhappy.

Yes, he may still go ahead and do whatever he wants to, but that cannot mean that you do not even try.

You mention that this has brought you closer to each other, that you are able to share so much more about your feelings, desires and fantasies. Once again, I want you to evaluate this carefully, because it seems that you are now even more afraid of sharing what you really feel. If you do indeed feel you are being able to speak more openly, this is something you should be able to say with confidence. If, as you say, it has brought you closer, you need to use that closeness to make him listen to your point of view.

But, and this is important, you also have the responsibility of being more honest about your feelings so that he understands what he needs to do.

From what you have said, he is trying to create a closeness and a special bond using what he perceives as mutual interest. He is trying to make sure that he does not make you feel jealous. As he has said, he is using the scenario to raise arousal (the woman in his office flirting with him) and then turning to you with that arousal. From the discussions that you seem to have had with him, he is doing the best he can to be the partner he thinks you want.

He is flourishing in this scenario – comfortable and stress-free in the knowledge that he can indulge his fantasies with honesty and openness and his wife's permission. You on the other hand are becoming more anxious, this is destroying your trust, and your insecurities are piling up.

You need to make this clear to him, along with all your concerns about the family, no matter how difficult it is. Because although you feel uncomfortable right now, there are no guarantees that you will not become emotionally involved with the next 'bull' – and that will cause more issues in the relationship.

This is a complicated situation and there will be no straightforward answers. Moreover, there are no precedents or notes you can refer to, to say this is what I need to do. It will need to be a process of trial and error and a huge amount of mature thinking.

What next?

Understand that you are allowed to say no. You don't need to justify or suppress how you feel. The discomfort, jealousy and fear you're experiencing are signals that something isn't working for you. Instead of questioning whether you have the 'right' to feel this way, accept that you do and that your emotions deserve attention.

Tell your husband clearly you do not want to continue down this path, that you're not comfortable with a threesome, nor an open or non-monogamous relationship. I know you are worried about what this may mean for your marriage, but honesty is going to give you a better chance of saving the marriage than keeping quiet about it.

Seek emotional support outside the relationship. You are carrying a heavy emotional load alone. Whether it's a therapist or a trusted friend, find a space where you can process your feelings without being judged. A professional might also help you navigate how to communicate your boundaries more effectively.

I want to finish by saying that I think you are a very capable, intelligent woman and you will understand how to make the right decision and follow through with it. When the conversation first came up, you gave it careful thought, weighed your own discomfort against what would make your partner happy. Similarly, you will find the strength and resolve to come to the decision you need to make.

I've been married for twelve years and have two kids; married life is fine. We recently became friends with another couple, and I have started developing feelings for the other lady. I haven't told her because I'm afraid I will lose the friendship if she doesn't like me. But I keep thinking of her. I like her dressing sense, her maturity, her mental clarity, and the way she handles life situations on her own, things I find lacking in my wife. Also, I feel sympathy towards her as I came to know that her husband hits her. Are these emotions normal? I don't even know what I want from this. Please guide me.

A 2010 study survey of 3000 couples found that nearly everyone, at some point, has experienced feelings for someone outside their marriage, whether they were bored or dissatisfied or content and deeply in love with their spouse. One in twenty-five admitted to being in love with someone else for several years, one in twenty said the same despite being in a happy relationship, and one in six confessed to having had an extramarital affair.

Among men, 22 per cent said they had loved two women at the same time, compared to 15 per cent of women who said they had loved two men at the same time. And 29 per cent of men said they had considered leaving their partner for the other woman compared to 19 per cent of women reporting similar intentions.

Feeling attracted to someone outside of your relationship is possibly the most common dilemma that monogamously committed couples face, and while it can come with its challenges it is neither unique nor rare and nor will it be a one-off event.

Attraction is a normal part of life. Being in a committed relationship does not make you immune to noticing or being drawn to others. It's not always about a deep connection or a grand, epic romance; sometimes it is just about chemistry, timing or curiosity. It is a natural human response and in most cases the feeling fades as it arrived.

That said, while attraction is involuntary, acting on it is always a choice. And how you respond to that choice can reshape your life in ways you may not expect.

Unfortunately, because even the thought of being attracted to someone else is seen as cheating, we never talk about sexual chemistry, which means we don't get the right kind of advice to deal with it, which in turns ends with pointless affairs, broken relations and a lot of unnecessary misery all around.

So here is my advice. When two people come into regular contact, share easy conversations and build familiarity, it's common for sexual tension to build. Especially if the new person seems to embody qualities you feel are missing in your partner.

You have said you admire things about this woman that you feel your wife lacks. It is far more possible, however, that these are things your wife just doesn't have the bandwidth to show you in the middle of raising children, managing a home and general domestic fatigue.

You are comparing someone you meet socially at her best public-facing self with your wife in her rawest, most exhausted moments. After twelve years of marriage, it is natural that everything about your partner may feel familiar, routine and unexciting, but it is not a fair comparison.

You also mentioned feeling sympathy for the other woman because her husband is abusive. That is deeply concerning but that pain is an excuse for romanticising the situation. Abuse needs to be addressed by helping her create a network of safety and support, not by creating another complicated emotional mess. Nobody needs to be part of a toxic emotional triangle.

You acknowledge you're afraid of losing her friendship if she does not feel the same way, but the greater risk is to your marriage and to your children's emotional world. The fallout of crossing this line can be far more destructive than you can imagine. Even if nothing physical happens, secrecy and emotional loyalty outside the marriage can start unravelling the relationship from within.

What next?

Do not compare your wife to someone new. Your wife is living with you in real time: unfiltered moments of vulnerability, parenting, exhaustion and routine arguments. Someone you see socially is presenting a version of herself that is curated and polished. Admiring that is natural, but comparing it to your spouse's daily life is unfair.

Do not justify an affair. Avoid falling into mental traps like 'she is in pain', 'my wife does not understand me', or 'monogamy is unnatural'. Instead, focus on why you should not act on it: 'I do not want to lose my family', 'this is not love, this is fantasy', 'once the line is crossed, I cannot go back'.

Set boundaries in your own head. Temptation begins in the mind. It might feel harmless, even exciting, to replay interactions, but all you are doing is reinforcing the attachment. Do not let your imagination linger. The first act of control happens there.

Focus on reconnecting with your partner before looking elsewhere for relief. All long-term relationships go through dull patches. If things are boring or stressful, address that. See what is missing or needs to be rebuilt.

Don't flirt – friend-zone. Do not spend time alone with this woman. Avoid long, private chats. Do not initiate physical contact. If needed, create some space to let the infatuation cool off.

Redirect your energy. Start a new hobby or sport, anything that challenges your mind or body. Often, infatuation grows in the vacuum of routine. Give yourself new stimuli so that your focus shifts from fantasy to action.

Being attracted to someone else is not a crisis. But acting on that attraction without clear thinking almost always is. What you are feeling may be common, but the consequences of following through are not. Make your decisions from clarity, not from sexual excitement. Your marriage, your family, and your peace of mind depend on it.

After 4 years of marriage my husband wants to be polyamorous. I want to be monogamous; sex is deeply emotional for me. He also admits he may not be comfortable seeing me with another man but he insists on being poly.

Do I have to accept it? He says it is not cheating because he has told me about it. I love him and don't want to leave him but what if he falls for someone else and leaves me? How can I trust he will be loyal? What should I do?

The term for a relationship where one partner desires monogamy and the other prefers polyamory is 'mono-poly'. Throughout history there have been mono-poly relationships where men of wealth and high standing had several wives and mistresses while women were expected to be monogamously faithful to the man to whom they 'belonged'. Over time and under social and religious dictums, heterosexuality and monogamy became the norm, making it the default relationship style.

Polyamory itself is a more modern term that came into circulation in the late twentieth century and was officially included in the Oxford English Dictionary in 2006, reflecting its growing cultural presence. Unlike 'polygamy', defined as one man with multiple wives, polyamory defines a relationship style based on what we call ethical non-monogamy, meaning both partners can make the decision to engage in romantic and/or sexual relationships with mutual consent.

Like all sexual orientations it is important to understand that monogamy and polyamory exist on a spectrum. Mono-poly relationships can vary from couples who may want to be 'monogamish' (where occasional non-monogamous experiences are permitted) to those who engage in full-fledged polyamory.

Let me start by saying that regardless of this vast spectrum of possibilities, not everyone is built for a mono-poly relationship. This isn't some hormone-fuelled free-for-all where you jump into bed with whoever you like. Polyamory demands a great deal of emotional maturity, a deep understanding of shifting boundaries, and an ongoing commitment to consent and communication.

For the partner wanting to explore polyamory, it's essential to create a safe, supportive environment. In many ways, the emotional constraints you take on to ensure your partner's comfort are far more demanding than those in monogamy.

Polyamory means different things to different people. For some, it's rooted in cultural tradition that historically frames it as a man's right and a woman's duty, which brings with it clear power imbalances. For others, especially in its modern, consensual definition, it is seen as an expansion of love, not a rejection of commitment. The idea here is that love is not a finite resource and so new relationships don't divide or subtract feelings, they add new ones.

Some people view polyamory as emotionally healthier because it relieves the pressure of one partner having to meet every single need. For others it gives them the sexual freedom they believe is necessary to their well-being.

But here's the catch – people don't just see polyamory differently, they practise it differently too. For example, in some polyamorous relationships, the primary partner (in this instance you, the wife) holds the most important place in your partner's life, while others are considered secondary. For others it may mean that all their partners are on an equal footing.

Some people practise full transparency, where everyone knows and may even interact with other partners. Others follow a 'don't ask, don't tell' model, where you know other people exist, but not who they are or how often they're seen. This is why it is essential to understand what polyamory means to both of you. Because when you start the conversation, you need to know you are both negotiating and navigating the same thing.

Then come the logistics. How will your husband divide time between the partners? Will there be different days for everyone or will it be based on hours? Where will he meet his other partners – at their home or yours? Will you have a veto power over future partners? Are you expected to eventually accept and build relationships with others, or is this a one-sided arrangement?

Now consider financial implications. If you share income, and he begins supporting others financially, how does that affect you? If he is going to contribute to another household, even occasionally, it will create a shortfall. You need to know what that shortfall is and how acceptable it feels.

Then there's what I call 'leftover energy syndrome'. If he spends the day in the excitement of a new partner, what is left for you by nightfall? If his best self is being poured into someone else, where does that leave you?

Then there's sexual health. If he's going to have multiple partners, you need new, clear, and completely non-negotiable protocols around regular STI testing, condom use, and honest updates.

Now to your fears: 'If I say no, will he do it anyway? And if he tells me, is it still cheating?'

Just because he's 'told you' doesn't mean he now has a free pass to do whatever he wants. The emphasis in ethical non-monogamy is ethical. Polyamory is about mutual agreements, which means your consent is paramount. If he moves ahead with other partners knowing you have not agreed to it, it is a breach of boundaries and does count as cheating. Disclosure is not the same as permission and you need to know this clearly when you have your conversation – it is not about being resigned to what he is going to do but to mutually agree on the best way forward.

And now possibly your greatest concern – what if he falls for someone else? I want you to understand that this is a very real fear. Even in ethically non-monogamous relationships, there is no guarantee that feelings won't deepen elsewhere. Polyamory as a theory believes that love isn't finite. But if your emotional well-being depends on being the one and only, that idea will never feel safe, no matter the reassurances.

So the more important question becomes 'what happens if he does fall for someone else?' What is he promising you in that case? And is that promise enough to help you feel secure? None of these are minor concerns, they are the foundation of your future well-being.

That you want to be monogamous and your husband does not is not just about having different sexual preferences, it's a fundamental contrast in how each of you see love and partnership. Ask yourself – what is it that truly distresses you about his desire for polyamory? Is it just that you've never thought of relationships as anything but monogamous or is it the fear of what people will think or the fear that you will not get the emotional bond that comes with being the only partner?

It could be that his desire for multiple partners is not about a lack of love for you but that doesn't mean your feelings are any less valid. They deserve to be heard, but for that it is essential you understand what you want and communicate it clearly – he is not a mind-reader.

It is not unusual for a monogamous partner to agree to polyamory, not because they want it, but because they are afraid of losing their partner. But that is not consent, it is coercion which tends quickly to turn to resentment. If monogamy is essential to you, you need to say so without feeling apologetic.

What next?

Clarify your position. Write down how you feel about polyamory, your fears, your boundaries, your emotional needs – and share them openly with your husband. He cannot respond to what you haven't clearly expressed.

Get detailed answers. Don't leave anything open-ended. Ask exactly what polyamory looks like to him. Where? With whom? How often? Will you meet these people? What happens if you say no?

Understand the difference between disclosure and consent. Just because he has 'informed' you does not mean you have agreed. If he acts without your consent, it is still a violation of trust.

Seek professional support. A relationship therapist who understands non-monogamy can help create a safe, neutral space for you to navigate these conversations.

Don't negotiate yourself out of your own needs. You're allowed to say no. You're allowed to want monogamy, even if he wants something else. Love does not mean abandoning yourself.

One of the hardest parts of mono-poly relationships is the constant tug-of-war between wanting to support your partner's freedom and needing to protect your own emotional well-being.

You may find yourself saying yes to polyamory because you want to be open-minded, or because you don't want to lose him. But somewhere in that process, you may start to feel you've lost yourself.

That's why open and clear communication matters. Make notes, ask him everything you need to know and tell him everything that is worrying you, listen to his responses and then decide – not based on fear but on what works for you equally.

And finally – it is difficult to accept but sometimes the differences are too deep to bridge. Love is not always enough. If your fundamental needs clash with his, staying in this relationship could mean years of resentment and emotional exhaustion and that's a cost no one should have to pay.

We have been married for 9 years but the spark in our sex life has faded. We live in a conservative joint family, so role play or toys are not really an option. My husband suggested trying a foot fetish because he read it can be very exciting, but we do not know much about it. I want to understand what a foot fetish involves. I read about Chinese foot binding, which sounds painful. How can we begin, any techniques you can suggest?

Feet have carried more erotic symbolism than almost any other body part, making foot fetishism, or sexual attraction to feet, one of the oldest and most practised of the erotic arts across cultures. Ancient Egyptian erotic papyri depict lovers kissing and caressing feet, while Victorian erotica is filled with references to boot-licking and toe-sucking.

The most well known of course are the Chinese erotic traditions, where the foot was considered so intimate that simply holding it was equated with sex itself, and the number of ways to engage with the foot was said to exceed the sexual positions in the *Kama Sutra*. Women were trained to undo a man's trousers with their toes, to take his penis between the arches of their feet, and to complete the act without ever using their hands – a technique more highly rated than penetrative sex. One highly sought-after form of foreplay involved a woman manipulating almonds between her toes and then feeding them to her lover. However, much of this was tied to the practice of foot-binding, a brutal form of control and subjugation, and that history must be clearly separated from consensual erotic traditions, which centre pleasure, not pain.

For instance, for the ancient Indians, the erotic power of the foot lay not in its captivity but in its movement. The dancer's foot was the ultimate tool of seduction, adorned with jewellery, ankles lengthened with ghungroos (bells), arches tinted with alta (red paste).

Today, foot fetishism remains one of the most common and widely practised kinks. For couples in conservative settings, it offers a discreet and equipment-free way to explore novelty and playful intimacy, without drawing unwanted attention.

Since both of you have already taken that first step of wanting to learn more, I'm going to walk you through what a foot fetish is and the different ways to approach it with privacy and pleasure and without any kind of awkwardness.

Foot play varies with individual taste. For some, the attraction is to the shape of the foot, for others, it could be about the arch, the toes, the heel, or even the soles. Some people are excited by the way the foot moves, others by how it's adorned, and some find the scent itself a trigger for arousal. You don't have to play along to any script; this can be completely your thing.

Also, don't feel intimidated by the vocabulary. Words like 'dominance' and 'submission' can sound intense, but for many people it is just to indicate who will be standing, sitting, kneeling, etc. You don't have to act out any dramatic roles. Filled with nerve endings, the foot is incredibly sensitive, so you can keep it completely vanilla and it will still be deeply erotic without getting wild.

Before you try anything, have an open conversation about what you are thinking of doing – what excites you, what you are open to, what is a definite no. Make a list of things you might try, and then mark them as 'yes', 'no', and 'maybe'. If you do decide to experiment with some kind of restraint or dominance, agree on a safe word or signal.

Then set your boundaries – this is important because one partner might want to go faster than the other. Decide if the feet will only be part of foreplay, will they stay below the waist, or are you both comfortable bringing them near the mouth? And remember, nothing is written in stone – if it doesn't feel good you can change your mind midway. Or even if it felt good this time but you don't want to try it again, that's OK too. Consent is ongoing, not a one-time agreement.

So where do you start?

Making sure that your feet have been well washed and cleaned, begin with something simple, like just holding and rubbing each other's feet. Note what it feels like to have your foot touched in different ways.

Use your thumbs and knuckles to massage warm oils over the arches, heels and toes. See if you can kiss or gently lick the sole. Use featherlight touches or try temperature play like ice cubes or warm towels to awaken different nerve endings.

You can also tease your partner using your feet. Stroke their leg with your toes or play footsie under the covers.

As you try each thing, tell each other what you are enjoying, what you want more of, when you want it slower, etc. It isn't always easy to relax into foot play, you might feel embarrassed or overly ticklish. The mantra here is relax and go slower.

The idea of foot play is to create a feeling of luxurious indulgence so it doesn't have to be directly sexual. Whatever you are doing, even if it is just a massage, focus on the sensations they create because that can really help build erotic anticipation.

If either of you feels awkward, begin fully clothed or in non-sexual settings, like a foot rub while watching TV. Talk after each attempt – what felt good, what felt strange, and what you'd like to do differently next time.

Avoid comparing yourselves to extreme versions you might have seen in porn or read about in history, like Chinese foot binding or fetishised extremes like toe penetration.

If you have hygiene worries, turn foot care into a shared ritual – pedicures, bath time foot scrubs, or massaging oils together.

For anyone wanting to explore foot play, here's a simple 'foot night' ritual to begin with.

Start by setting the scene. Use oils, candles, soft lighting, and music to create a calm, inviting mood. Add a touch of luxury by adorning the feet. You can use anklets, toe rings, or just a little perfumed oil to draw attention to them. To increase focus on sensation rather than thought, you might introduce a blindfold. A soft scarf or any comfortable fabric will work. You can also add a gentle element of restraint by loosely tying the hands together.

Step by step
The receiver lies down, either on their back or on their stomach. They can choose whatever position feels more relaxing.

If you're using restraints, tie the hands lightly with something like a scarf. They can be positioned above the head or at the sides, depending on what feels secure and comforting – this is not about control or violence, it's about enhancing trust through vulnerability.

If you're adding a blindfold, this will help the receiver become more aware of the sensations they're feeling.

The giver then turns their full attention to the feet. Use slow, deliberate touch – massaging movements, kissing the toes, running the tip of your tongue along the arch, or even tracing an ice cube around the heel.

The goal is not to build quickly towards climax – you're simply creating anticipation while making the feet the centre of sensual awareness.

When both of you are comfortable, you can introduce playful elements like gentle commands or role play. You could also include kissing, soft biting or placing the feet on the giver's chest or face.

The best part of this practice is that it turns every touch into a ritual, the slowness of it makes you feel very aware and present, something that often gets lost in everyday sex.

Positions and play ideas

If you enjoyed the ritual, here are some simple positions that highlight the feet. These help build closeness and excitement, and they don't require any special equipment.

- *The cradle kiss.* One partner lies on their back with knees bent as the other sits near their feet, holding, kissing or massaging the feet and ankles. This position is great for adding oral stimulation if you want it.
- *The foot throne.* One partner sits on a chair or the edge of the bed. The other lies on their back with their feet resting in the seated partner's lap or on their chest. This is a great way to have a relaxed conversation about what all you did during the day while also making it deeply intimate.
- *Anklet adoration.* While in missionary, lift and play with the partner's foot, kissing or stroking the ankle and toes. It is a great way to add variety to what can become quite a routine position.
- *Inter-foot teasing.* Feet are used like hands. Place a foot on your partner's chest, stroke their thigh with your toes, or gently cup their genitals with your arches. This works well whether you're clothed or naked.

I do not know what this relationship is – or if it is even a relationship. He never calls me first. He never texts unless he wants to meet. He never stays the night. He is never around when I need him, and when I tell him I feel like he is using me, he says I am being too emotional and ruining a 'good thing'. But the moment he messages me again, I go running. I always say I will not, but I do. I get excited, I get dressed, I tell myself maybe this time it will feel different. And after it is over, I just feel stupid and low. I do not even think he likes me that much – I think he just likes that I am available. But I cannot seem to say no to him. I do not know how to get out of this or even if I want to. What does this even mean?

Unfortunately, this has always been the woman's role in relationships – 'to wait' for affection, for attention, for marriage, and to be available whenever it is offered. In our mothers' time, it was framed as 'her duty'; in the 1970s and 1980s, it became about how you 'kept him interested'; and today it is repackaged as being 'trendy, cool and commitment-free' because this is what makes you more desirable.

But underneath it all, the message remains the same – women's emotional and physical availability is expected but rarely reciprocated. The consistent message is that emotional restraint is a virtue. Asking for clarity or commitment makes you 'too needy', 'too clingy', or 'too much', that is, undesirable, whereas tolerating his inconsistencies means you are chill and mature, and hence the perfect partner.

As a result, women learn to question their own boundaries rather than men's behaviour. Eventually, the desire to be 'chosen' by him, within this imagined version of the relationship, becomes stronger than their instinct to protect themselves, and the longer they stay in this kind of relationship, the more they begin to believe that this is what intimacy should feel like – unpredictable, unequal, and just out of reach.

I call it the 'wind chime effect'. Much like a wind chime that is decorative but immobile, completely dependent on the wind to fulfil its purpose – only when the wind blows can it move, make a sound, and become everything it has the potential to be. Similarly, women are taught to be decorative, available, and silently in waiting, only to be activated when 'chosen' for attention.

The word for this is situationship.

You are not being weak or dramatic, you are confused because you are tangled up in a situation that is designed to keep you confused. You think you're in love, not with him but what you think he might become, and you keep retuning because your brain desperately wants to believe that there is the possibility of something more, that one day he will suddenly realise how much he loves you and the 'waiting' will have been worth it.

At some point you have to separate the 'hope' from the evidence. If someone keeps telling you that you are 'ruining a good thing' when you express your needs, it is not a relationship, it is emotional gaslighting disguised as a 'good thing'.

What next?

The first thing is to understand how to say a firm no. You don't have to take drastic steps or delete his number or pretend you care less. You just need to give yourself time to recognise that your yes is not coming from desire but from habit, fear, and a wild hope.

And yes, it will mean that you must distance yourself for a bit. Not to teach him a lesson or prove a point, but to interrupt the cycle. At the moment, the 'relationship' is like an ever-spinning loop that is blurring the vision. You need to stop long enough to see the road signs.

Next, draw a line between fantasy and reality. Each time you respond (in the hope that this time will be different), you are training yourself to tolerate neglect in the name of romance. You have begun to believe that the way he treats you is somehow a reflection of your worth and that has you clinging to the fantasy even harder, because if one day he turns around and says he cannot live without you, it will be proof that you were always 'special'.

Ditch the shame. Your inability to leave him is not a 'flaw', it's just the pattern you're now accustomed to – when he goes silent you feel distraught, when he sends a message your energy rushes back. We all function on emotional rhythms and you have become attuned to this rhythm – all we need to do is change the tuning.

Having said that, I think it's also important to address your responsibility in this. People *know* when something is terribly wrong but choose to override their instincts and friends' concerns, and keep insisting 'he is different' – even as he repeatedly shows you he is not – as an excuse to stay.

Tell one person the truth. Not the version where you say 'it's complicated' or 'we're just seeing how it goes'. Tell someone the truth of what's happening. There is immense power in saying it out loud.

Maybe you went into this relationship saying you were OK with something casual and no strings attached. Maybe it was true at the time. Till one day, as it often happens, you caught feelings.

Changing your mind is not shameful and falling in love is not a weakness, but it does come with the responsibility of recognising when the relationship no longer aligns with what you want. Clinging on endlessly is what makes it a truly toxic place to be in, because the longer you stay, the more you invest, and the harder it becomes to leave without feeling like the failure is yours.

Situationships pull you in precisely because they seem like the 'perfect solution'. They give you just enough to stay invested, which stops you from recognising that it is never going to be enough. And they often continue far longer than they should because we confuse their intensity with real connection.

Wanting to feel secure is not a personality flaw and it definitely does not make you 'clingy', just as being 'chill' is not the flex that most people think it is. You are allowed to admit that this isn't what you signed up for, even if you once said you were OK with it.

And pulling yourself out of the loop to look for clarity is the only way to do it.

Recently, at a party my best friend's boyfriend hit on me. It was dark and we were all sitting together on the sofa when he tried to touch me inappropriately. When I confronted him, he broke down and began to justify his actions saying he did it because he believed both of us were unhappy in our respective relationships. I feel disgusted and violated.

I made him tell his girlfriend, who was understandably distraught, and despite my own pain, I consoled her.

However, in an unexpected turn of events, she reconciled with him and completely cut me out of her life without any explanation or apology. I feel betrayed, abandoned, and punished for being the victim of his actions. I find myself questioning if I did the right thing, whether I could have handled it differently, or if I somehow deserve this isolation.

How do I cope with the trauma and the betrayal from people I considered close friends? How do I make peace with myself and rebuild my sense of self-worth?

Sexual assault within friend groups is one of the most silencing forms of trauma. In many social circles, especially tight-knit ones, victims are not only expected to minimise the incident, they are often punished for disrupting the group's perceived harmony. Standing up against the problem makes you the problem and loyalty to romantic partners is frequently prioritised over accountability so that the weight of the entire situation ends up falling on the person who was violated. Because we are conditioned to believe that bad behaviour is not the problem, disturbing the 'happy' veneer is.

What happened to you was not a misunderstanding, it was assault. Someone you trusted crossed a boundary he had no right to and then tried to excuse his actions with spurious justifications, as though anything could be an excuse for violating consent. It was made worse by the fact that it happened in a room full of people you should have felt safe around.

You did the right thing by confronting him and insisting on honesty, even though it has backfired. His girlfriend, in deciding that it was your presence and not his behaviour that was the problem, has fallen into the societal trope of learned behaviours around women being competitive.

This is a skewed pattern. You'll notice that men often support each other unconditionally, sometimes at the expense of truth and justice. If a man claims that another man's wife or partner made an advance, his word is generally taken at face value, and the woman is blamed.

Conversely, women have been conditioned to view each other as competitors, especially in the context of romantic relationships. This internalised misogyny leads to a belief that securing and maintaining a romantic relationship is paramount, even if it means losing a close friend or disregarding their trauma – female friendships are seen as dispensable while romantic partnerships become indispensable.

Societal narrative often paints the woman as the 'slut' or the one at fault, making it easier to doubt her than to confront the uncomfortable truth about a male partner's misconduct. Unfortunately, many women recognise these patterns only after multiple incidents, by which time significant damage has been done.

Your friend's decision to reconcile with him and cut you off is a manifestation of these deep-seated societal biases. It's a painful betrayal, but it's not a reflection of your worth or the validity of your experience. People would rather pretend nothing happened than face the discomfort of knowing someone they love could do something like this.

You need someone in your corner to tell you that you did everything right. You called it out, you drew your boundary, you told the truth – that is real strength.

When a woman is strong, especially in the aftermath of a sexual violation, it often makes others uncomfortable.

What you are now facing is the shame that survivors are so often left with, because no one else wants to hold space for what was done to them. And that is made worse by the loss of a friendship – we are guided through breakups, but no one teaches us how to process the loss of a friendship even though (I think) it is far more traumatic.

What next?

It feels tough right now, and possibly even awkward around the friends' group, but you do need to distance yourself from individuals who do not respect or believe you. So long as you have a couple of people who support you, you will find the strength to be OK.

Recognise that confronting this guy and insisting on honesty was very brave; it would have been much easier to stay silent. You chose not to betray your friend despite the difficult position you have been put in.

Your experience and feelings are valid. Healing is a journey, acknowledge your tears and your hurt, and tell yourself it is OK to seek help and take the time you need to recover.

Me and my partner have started our relationship directly in LDR, knowing that we can't meet for at least a year with a time difference of 7.5 hrs. I want your suggestion on how we can bond with each other emotionally and through physical attraction, more and more without making our relationship fall apart.

A long-distance relationship (LDR) might be seen as a modern inconvenience, but as a concept it has existed forever – wars that could last decades, merchants stuck on long and unknown trade routes, young men sent away to apprentice, study, or serve in foreign courts, colonial officials working abroad, maintaining ties with families they rarely saw, and even the tradition of long and strenuous pilgrimages that demanded time and solitude.

Distance has always been part of relationship structures, but today LDRs are more common than ever. And while technology makes staying connected easier, there are still the challenges of time zone differences, loneliness, miscommunication, emotional insecurity, safety concerns, and financial strain, alongside the complications of building and maintaining intimacy from a distance.

At the same time, without physical distraction and from sheer necessity, long-distance couples often learn to build stronger communication habits and emotional insights that sustain the relationship better in the long term.

Starting a relationship long distance, knowing you will not meet for at least a year and managing a 7.5-hour time difference, is hard. It will take commitment, imagination, and emotional resilience. But it is entirely possible to build something deep and lasting, even from afar. The goal is not just to survive the distance but to grow stronger through it.

Possibly the most fundamental thing to understand is that 'closeness' is not about talking constantly – it's about feeling like you matter in each other's daily lives. Whether that means sending a photo of the view from your window or a quick voice note about something that made you laugh or just telling your partner you tried a new recipe, the idea is not to be just a 'caller' but to actually participate in each other's lives.

The time difference means you will need to be intentional about when and how you connect. Choose two fixed 'date chats' in the week, where you set aside time to talk without distractions. Dress up, eat a meal together, and chat – treat it like a proper date. This is far more meaningful than forcing daily conversations or feeling pressure to be constantly available, which can very quickly build into resentment, impatience, and that 'tone'.

Another practical way to stay connected is to plan a shared activity that both of you can do in your own space so that you can compare the experience when you speak next.

This creates the feeling of enjoying things together even while apart, at the same time making it a familiar experience for when you are together, something that you have already bonded over.

Stay grounded in your own friendships, hobbies, routines, and passions. Do not let the relationship become your only source of connection. A fulfilling LDR needs two strong individuals, not two people waiting for time to pass.

Be prepared for difficult moments. Some days will feel impossible. There will be fights, insecurities, or sadness. Recognise it's not a crisis, just a moment, and the moment will pass. Vulnerability is part of intimacy. But your partner cannot always fix it, and you cannot expect them to. This is where you learn to listen, to ask for comfort, and to give it without pressure.

Mutual masturbation over video can be incredibly intimate, as long as it is consensual, discussed in advance, and emotionally safe. Make clear agreements about privacy and trust. Erotic desire thrives when emotional safety is intact. Without it, people shut down.

And now for the biggest challenge – unfulfilled physical desire.

This is often where LDRs begin to crack. Phone sex gets repetitive, sexting can feel flat, so this is where you need to get most creative.

Desire is not just physical, it is about imagination and anticipation. Tell each other what you want to do when you meet. Create stories together. Share erotic content, describe sensations, and be curious about what excites the other person.

Activity

The erotic story exercise.

This technique involves creating an erotic space together that can be part real, part fantasy to help couples explore intimacy at their own pace without the pressure of constantly 'performing on camera' or exchanging 'explicit' conversations on demand.

Step 1. Have the conversation

Fix a date to explore something intimate together. Make sure both of you are in a right headspace, with no time pressure or risk of interruption.

Step 2. Set boundaries

Agree on what is off-limits. Are intimate photos involved? Is it OK to reference other people, kinks, or fantasies outside the relationship? How will you signal if you want to pause or stop?

Step 3. Create your story

Pick a setting – real or imagined. One person begins, 'We're by the lake. The only light is from the moon. I lean forward and stroke your thigh ...' The other responds, adding a few lines. Go back and forth, building the scene together. It can be steamy, sexy, vanilla, or funny – as you wish. The goal is not to 'perform', it is to create desire together. To make it 'steamier', add sensory details like scents and sounds, how their skin feels under your hand.

Step 4. Add a timer to pace arousal

Set a 1–2 minute timer to take turns telling the story. This creates a sense of edging – if the fantasy is building towards climax, the interruption holds you just short, turning the story from mental play into foreplay. Not knowing exactly when the timer will go off also keeps you from trying to say the 'right thing' and keeps you following your desire instead.

Step 5. Pillow talk

Afterwards, talk about it. What surprised you? What felt exciting, awkward, or emotionally risky? The after-sex chat often gets missed in LDRs; use this conversation to build sexual and emotional awareness.

Step 6. Next date

Treat the story as a thread you can return to. Revisit it, build on it, or develop characters and shared scenarios that evolve over time. This turns it from a one-off activity into an ongoing erotic connection.

Warning: Avoid saving sensitive content in shared cloud backups or on work devices.

Me and wife are now in our late 40s. Around twelve years back, we had some trouble in our marriage and agreed on introducing a third person in our lives and bedroom. First, it was soft threesomes, then it was full blown physicality. Slowly, as was expected, they became lovers even behind my back and I was eased out. Strange part is that I am a full-blooded male, but in that threesome relationship, I became a submissive partner to both. More than participating, it was watching them that started exciting me. My whole perception changed and the only thing that excites me today is the thought of my wife with him. It is like I have started feeling her through him.

I even write a diary for my self-arousal, where I act and feel like her and explain in detail my encounters with him.

For the record, I am a normal straight man with a good profile.

Is there any reason for this behaviour, which is a mixture of cuckold and voyeur? Is it mentioned in any ancient texts around the world?

You feel you are living a contradiction, of being a straight man whose arousal now depends entirely on the thought of the pleasure your wife feels with another man. What started as a threesome has changed to cuckoldry and voyeurism, where you no longer want to participate, only to watch. But even the 'watching' is not passive, you have started feeling her through him as you try to replicate that intensity of pleasure that you imagine she feels in those moments. Your arousal has shifted entirely into her experience, not just in fantasy but in actually restructuring your own erotic imagination to embody her.

According to Roy Baumeister's theory on masochism and erotic submission,* fantasies like cuckoldry and voyeurism

---

* Roy Baumeister is a social psychologist best known for his research on self-control, willpower and the psychology of sexuality.

are not signs of humiliation or dysfunction, rather they are temporary escapes from the role that has been carved out for them. He says that often men in high-responsibility roles can experience psychological exhaustion from constantly needing to lead, decide and perform, and erotic submission offers relief by allowing them to surrender control and step out of their dominant identity. Cuckoldry and voyeurism are not necessarily about inadequacy, it can equally be about letting go of pressure and performance and enjoying intimacy without the burden of leading.

It is not a sign of weakness, it is a coping mechanism that helps some people regulate their internal world.

So whether you are straight or not, let's start by saying that there is no single version of male sexuality and there is no fixed orientation for arousal. Just because at one point being the 'doer' was what excited you does not mean that you will always remain aroused by the same things. It evolves based on emotional context, experience, power dynamics and imagination. That you now prefer to watch or imagine rather than 'do' is not abnormal. It is simply how your desires have shifted.

The idea that 'straight masculinity' means always dominating or leading in bed is a warped patriarchal narrative, not biology or psychology. Wanting to watch, to submit, to eroticise your partner's pleasure through fantasy is far more common than you would believe. And it doesn't make you 'less of a man'. On the contrary your brain has managed to break through the rigid rules that dictate how men are *supposed* to experience arousal, to actually being able to tap into what really turns you on, no matter how frighteningly different it may seem.

Arousal is complicated.

Going back to the psychology behind cuckoldry and voyeurism, it is not always about humiliation or being dominated, despite what stereotypes suggest. In this case, the act of watching or imagining yourself in your wife's place is not about wanting to become her or about feeling him through her – this sounds more like you wanting to connect with a version of pleasure that feels unavailable to you.

You see an intensity or fulfilment in her experience – feeling desired, surrendering without pressure or control – that you have never been taught to claim for yourself, so you are now trying to imagine her pleasure in a way that you can inhabit as well. This is not about your sexuality, it just means that your erotic imagination does not fit neatly into the standard definitions, and that is not a problem (see Chapters 28 and 30).

You mentioned that this shift happened after the breakdown of your marriage. That detail matters. Sometimes, when a relationship ruptures, people try to reattach themselves through fantasy – fantasy becomes a tool to reorganise the relationship, especially when the ending was unresolved.

You are not just processing the loss of the relationship but also trying to understand how you have changed within it. The fantasy lets you play out scenarios that help you identify what keeps you connected, what still excites you and what no longer aligns with how you both are in the relationship.

So let's start by removing the question of whether you are 'normal'. Your arousal pattern is not uncommon. Our ancient texts are full of stories of emotional and physical role reversal, of fantasy and imagination and how the erotic power of 'witnessing' is an important factor in arousal.

What matters more is whether it feels healthy and sustainable or is it making you feel stuck and ashamed. If it feels fulfilling and honest, there is no need to change anything. But if you find that you are clinging to fantasy because real connection feels unavailable, then you need to work on that because this will just act as surface Band-Aid.

Also, understand that this arousal pattern doesn't define you, it is just one part of your sexual self. It may stay, it may change again. Adding labels is just likely to cause tension rather than solve anything.

Can you create a very specific and dedicated, detailed vlog about how couples can smoothly build up mood on weekdays if either or both have a very stressful work environment. It can have ideas and tips about how the man/woman can de-stress and disconnect mentally from work after returning home in a manner which can prepare/flow the mind's thoughts and body's freshness and do some things with their partner to build the mood towards lovemaking in the night.

We know that relationships need real work to keep things fresh, but that's easier said than done. Real life is about daily routines, professional stress, mental exhaustion, small arguments and unspoken irritations. There are parents to take care of, bills to pay, groceries to buy, deadlines to meet. And in the middle of all this, you are expected to maintain a secure, emotionally stable relationship and somehow cultivate a high-energy, imaginative sex life.

That is a lot. And it is not always possible to sustain it all at once.

It is, however, possible to build small, realistic habits that help reconnect you with your partner sexually, emotionally and mentally. According to the *Kama Sutra* the secret lies in knowing how to transition from the chaos of the day into moments of connection.

There is no fixed formula or weekly schedule that will guarantee closeness or arousal but here is a list of transition rituals that I use. Remember it's not about 'having sex', it's about building up the desire and space to 'want it'. Because that's what will keep the connection intact.

The *Kama Sutra* says that even before beginning foreplay partners should spend cuddles time together exchanging naughty or gossipy stories in order to shift their headspace from the stresses of the day to each other, because only when you are mentally and emotionally together can it lead to good sex. I think it's not just for sex but this is equally valuable as a daily connection ritual: 15–20 minutes of screen-free closeness. Some days this can be playful and flirtatious, meant to lead to something; on others it can simply be a way to talk about your day to de-stress and connect.

Importantly, don't turn this into a to-do task, let it be your comfort moment that you look forward to, that your day would feel incomplete without.

In the spirit of not just 'having sex' but building the desire to do so, it is important to have lots of shared non-sexual activities.

Couple of times in the week cook together – it's what I call relationship foreplay – either just a simple meal or add some fun by turning it into a game. Watch comedy together. Being able to laugh together builds a bond that is second only to good sex. Singles clubs are now recommending hiking or gardening days instead of candlelit dinners as a far better way of connecting – do a shared outdoor activity. Spend an evening side by side doing your own thing, being together without the pressure to talk to each other – companionable silence can be deeply intimate. But equally, make space for quality time apart. Do fun engaging things with friends, colleagues or on your own so you return to each other with fresh energy, new stories and a relationship that continues to feel interesting and alive.

But while all of this is essential for emotional closeness, it can also tip the relationship into just feeling like friendship, and equally if the goal each time is sex, that pressure quickly kills desire.

So at the end of each day, take 15 minutes to cuddle skin-to-skin and talk about the day – work, activities, problems, everything but with no agenda and no pressure for sex. This is not 'sexy time', this is 'intimate comfort' time, where the aim is simply to stay emotionally connected and to remind yourselves of how good it feels to rest in each other's arms, because when intimacy begins to fade, the first thing we forget is the comfort of the other's bare skin against our own.

And on nights when desire feels far away, and even cuddling feels too performative, try lying down together fully clothed, and just spoon for 10 minutes. No talking, no goal, just comfort as the baseline from which arousal can slowly return without pressure.

Another favourite of mine is the 'Tell me something you noticed about me this week' game. It could be as simple as 'You looked great in that old T-shirt' or 'I noticed how patient you were on that call'. It takes hardly any time or effort but effectively pulls you out of 'routine mode'. On low-energy days, this small ritual is a reminder that you are appreciated.

Flirt but in a cheeky and fun way, not sexual – 'You looked smug with that coffee this morning', or 'I saw the way you stretched show off'. This helps both partners stay tuned into desire as a background rhythm. Or try a micro-date, like maybe a shared coffee outside the house. Often, it can do more for your connection than a long, expensive dinner.

What keeps intimacy alive is not performance, it is connection. Some days you may need to reconnect through silence, other days through shared laughter or play. Some evenings are meant for mellow, non-sexual touch; others need energy.

My wife and I have been together for about 3 years. We met through a girl who is like my sister, she ties rakhi on me, puts Bhai Dooj tikka, etc. Last year, we all went for a beach vacation. Both girls were holding my arms and splashing and playing. My sister's breasts were pressing into my arm, which made me a little uncomfortable but in that moment I got a slight hard-on. I kept trying to switch places, to put my girlfriend (now wife) between us, but they kept pulling me back into the middle. Eventually, I forgot about it.

Last month, I told my wife about that incident during a moment of vulnerability. I made it clear it was unintentional and something I never acted on. But my wife, who is already a little insecure about her smaller breasts, has not been able to let it go. She now says, 'You cannot be my man if you are affected by other women.' I regret bringing it up, but I was being honest and trusting her not to judge me.

How do I help her understand that this was not cheating? That I love her deeply, and this was not a conscious or chosen reaction? I am scared this might tear our marriage apart.

Arousal non-concordance is a word that should be in everyone's sexual health vocabulary. It means that arousal is not always about attraction and neither is it always a conscious decision. The body is wired to react to certain stimuli, and often it is just the brain recognising that pattern. This is why victims of abuse are often wrongly blamed because if their body responded it is taken to mean 'they wanted it'.

Erections specifically can occur from all sorts of non-sexual and unlikely situations, like the vibrations from driving over a bumpy road, or from fear, or even in half sleep.

But unfortunately, between the guilt and shame we are taught to feel around our bodies and that no one ever explains these responses, the anxiety and self-blame that we carry feels far heavier than it deserves.

What happened in that moment at the beach was not a fantasy playing out. It was just your body reacting to a specific touch. It was an awkward moment, it passed and it was forgotten.

The real problem lies in how the conversation unfolded. You shared it in a moment of vulnerability because, as I mentioned, the body's involuntary sexual responses often leave us feeling ashamed, and so you felt this would be the 'honest' thing to do. But she heard it through the lens of her own insecurity.

Women are conditioned to view their bodies as a 'losing competition', to constantly compare ourselves to other women, to notice that we fall short and then to measure our worth through that comparison. We are also taught that erection means 'attraction'. So no matter how much you insist it was meaningless, to her it is proof of her supposed 'shortcomings'. And when she says 'you cannot be my man if you are affected by other women', her anxiety is that she is not 'enough' for you. And this is what needs to be addressed.

The *Kama Sutra*, in a chapter on lovers' quarrels, says, 'If the man offends his partner by taking the name of another woman during intercourse, he must immediately apologise without pride or hesitation. He must do so repeatedly and humbly, without argument or justification, until she is fully pacified and returns to him of her own accord.'

The emphasis is that the 'making up' must come from a place of complete emotional generosity without ego or defensiveness or logic because not only does this heal, but through this she will end up loving him even more than before. This is one of those moments.

It may feel unfair or exhausting, especially when you know that it meant nothing, but this is where your response matters most. If she's looking for assurance that you love her for herself and not measured against someone else's body, assure her. Tell her what you notice most about her, what you love about being with her, what makes her attractive to you that goes far beyond breasts or bodies. There is no quick fix for emotional insecurity, but patient reassurance without irritation can lay the foundation for deeper trust going forward.

But equally lay down your boundaries. You don't have to keep proving your innocence, you did nothing wrong. Explain that you shared that memory not because it meant anything, but because you never wish to hide things from her that could lead to misunderstandings later. The problem is that people often ask for honesty in a relationship, but do not know how to receive it without getting defensive and turning it into blame.

You were honest about a vulnerable moment, and that takes courage. But when honesty is met with rejection or punishment, it becomes harder to stay open. So you now need to shift the focus, from trying to prove your innocence to setting boundaries around how both of you handle uncomfortable truths. So just as she has the right to feel reassured, you have the right to feel safe in your honesty. But that safety must come through everyday connection, not just after a fight. Because if you only return to 'stability' after a fight, the relationship ends up depending on fights to feel anchored.

We have been married 10 years with a new baby. My husband loves and supports me, including in front of his parents.

Recently, we shifted to a new home and there is a 17-year-old girl who's started liking my husband, which I was not aware of. She had taken his number in front of me saying that she needs some help for their house. My husband is a very jovial person. Later, she started texting him on Snapchat. He showed it to me and I said it's OK, just text back casually.

But then she started saying that she likes him, she can't live without him. My husband came and told me everything. I told him to block her and don't engage, she's only 17, it can cause other problems.

I thought he had done that because I didn't hear anything more for a week. But a couple of weeks later my husband came and apologised because he had hidden the truth from me. Instead of blocking, he began avoiding her and she got so mad she called him and said she had taken poison, to come and meet her immediately or she would die. My husband got scared and rushed to meet her without my knowledge.

She hugged and kissed him in public. My husband didn't react much because of her age, just asked her to stop and then dropped her home. But he didn't tell me at the time because I was under pressure from my office and new baby. He was still talking to that girl for a week on Snapchat after I asked him to stop. The girl also has become normal and apologised to me for what she did but this has really disturbed me. I feel like I was cheated. And although my husband has apologised many times, I feel I cannot trust him any more.

My life has turned into hell. We were such a loving couple and now it is all gone. Help me out of this trauma.

This is one of those situations where there is no simple right or wrong. Every action between the two of you came from a place of love and yet things have gone badly wrong. It's been a strong marriage based on trust. When a young girl asked for your husband's help, you made the decision together in good faith to share his number. When she started texting him he showed you the texts, everything was still open and honest.

But when the situation escalated, instead of blocking her as you had jointly decided, he felt that quietly avoiding her would work, and when that situation became more complicated he hid it from you in the belief that he was protecting you from unnecessary stress. And in doing so he has ended up creating exactly the stress, mistrust and pain he had wanted to save you from.

Your sense of betrayal is valid. Trauma is not just about what 'happens', it is how it leaves you feeling, how it makes everything that once felt safe suddenly unstable. When this girl began texting inappropriately and you asked him to block her, you were not just being jealous about another woman 'liking' your husband, it was the legal vulnerability that made this so dangerous. This was a 17-year-old-girl – the damage to your reputation, stability and your child's future could have been enormous. So, although this was not an 'affair' in the traditional sense, it was a deliberately unthinking act that could have ended really badly and that is what has left you wondering whether your relationship is really what you thought it was. Having said that, your husband also unwittingly found himself in an impossible position when the girl threatened to harm herself. Most people have no idea how to respond to something like this, and aside from the very real fear of someone getting hurt, being named in a suicide attempt can leave you in a police mess that can go on for years and ruin your life. So, it is understandable that he panicked.

Whatever his reasons for continuing to engage with her after you had both agreed that he shouldn't, his decision to not tell you came from a genuine desire to protect you which unfortunately backfired badly.

The girl's behaviour was completely unacceptable and inappropriate and I wish there were concrete ways to hold people accountable for such behaviour, because it can be extremely destructive for everyone involved. In theory it is very simple to say that adults should understand how to draw clear boundaries and disengage, but in reality when someone is threatening suicide, stepping back safely becomes far more complicated.

Most of us want to be good neighbours and be there to help the community, especially when it comes to younger people. But when that support spirals into something manipulative and unpredictable, most people are unprepared. It's safe to say that whatever his original intentions in not blocking her, his subsequent responses came from fear and confusion, not attraction.

What next?
None of this means your marriage is over. There is a crack in the relationship and rebuilding it will take time and effort but it is definitely possible.

On your husband's part he will need to take responsibility for his own choices – without defensiveness. But equally you have to take the responsibility of telling him what you need him to do in order to make this OK again – do you want full openness around his phone, do you want him to commit to couples counselling or will it need certain ground rules? Because he could keep trying to do what he thinks is best to fix the situation, but if that's not what you need, it will not help.

My advice would be to start with setting clear, non-negotiable boundaries around online and offline interactions going forward. Private online messaging is often seen as harmless because it is not 'physical', but the consequences can be very real – what starts casually can escalate quickly, as it did here.

Come to an agreement on what kind of contact with other women is appropriate, and make sure those boundaries are unambiguous. This is not about control, it is about restoring the sense of safety and partnership that has been damaged.

Dating as a single parent

With changing relationship structures, more single parents are re-entering the dating world. But dating when one has children is not as simple as just 'finding someone'. It means navigating guilt, loyalty, societal judgement and the pressure to prove you are still a 'good parent', while reassuring your child they remain your priority. Because when a parent starts dating, it changes the emotional landscape for everyone at home and there is nothing straightforward about that.

In the immediate aftermath of a breakup most people go through a familiar cycle. The rebound syndrome is very real. Many deal with the grief and confusion and stress of solo parenting – work, childcare, managing everything alone – by rushing into a new relationship. We begin searching for 'the one' because the urge is to replicate what was lost, to prove we are still desirable, rather than take time to ask what we truly need.

Which is why the first step is not to seek another relationship but to give yourself the space to date casually – to reconnect with your own desires, confidence and sexuality to understand what you want for yourself.

Once settled, decide whether you want to continue with occasional adult company or a long-term partner. This is not about the 'right' or 'wrong' reasons and you can change your mind at any time, but this is a great starting point to help you understand how much time you want to give a new partner, how much to involve your children and to communicate expectations.

Next comes the question of when and whether to tell your children. With younger kids, there is no need to bring up casual dating unless the relationship becomes serious. With teens, secrecy can backfire. They usually sense when something is happening, and being 'kept out' can breed resentment.

Relationship Structures

A few tips for this talk
- You are not asking for permission, you're keeping communication open.
- Don't get deep into it, just a simple 'I am spending time with someone I like, but I will only introduce you if it becomes something meaningful' can go a long way.
- The word 'meaningful' is better than 'serious' and presenting this as one part of your life (not its centre) makes it less threatening.

If the relationship does begin to move forward, consider putting a confidante in place for your child, someone you both trust, who can be a sounding board when emotions flare up. Children need a safe place to express frustration, especially in the early stages of adjustment, and this person should be someone who has your back.

Hold off on introductions until the relationship has shown stability. When you do arrange a meeting, choose a neutral, low-pressure activity, like a walk or a film, and keep it short. This is not about romantic displays but about easing into the idea.

Two things to remember
- Children take time to adjust, and you are not asking them to approve, only to meet someone you like.
- Emotional safety matters, and you should never let them form bonds with someone likely to disappear.

Children's reactions vary with age. Younger ones may cling more, while teens may turn sarcastic or withdrawn. Sons, in particular, may feel more protective or threatened by a new man in the home. But this is less about gender and more about how secure they feel with you. Reinforce that bond rather than rushing them into accepting someone new.

There is also the unfortunate truth of how society views dating parents – it depends heavily on gender. Single mothers are judged more harshly. A woman seeking love or even pleasure is often seen as selfish, while men are more likely to be praised for 'moving on'. This judgement is real, but your focus should remain on how you manage your relationship with your child. You cannot control society, but you can control how you create safety and openness at home.

Sometimes children are openly hostile to the person you are dating. Listen carefully. Is it about personality clashes – is your new partner too loud, too quiet, too different? Or have they behaved in a way that felt dismissive or overfamiliar? Or is it just fear of being replaced? Let your child express their feelings, but set boundaries. Rudeness is not acceptable. They do not have to like your partner, but they must show basic respect.

Do not stop dating to prove your loyalty. Emotional blackmail is real, especially when children feel insecure. 'You love them more than me' or 'You are breaking up the family' are common accusations. And if your ex is not moving on, they may be fuelling that resentment. Younger children may even fall sick more often or cry when you leave. These moments are painful, but giving in teaches the child that punishing your happiness gives them control. You can love your child completely and still have a life of your own.

One particularly sensitive issue is when a new partner tries to weigh in on your parenting. Unless they are committed and involved in daily life, they do not get a say in how you raise your child. Even if they mean well, even if the comments are coming from concern, not control, it is up to you once again to set the boundaries and the tone. The final decision about your child must always remain yours.

Finances need serious clarity. In the early stages, keep everything separate. If you are spending on dating, use a dedicated budget that does not touch your family's main funds. If the relationship becomes serious, have a clear conversation about how shared costs will be managed, especially when children are involved. Do not assume emotional closeness translates into financial support. If both of you have children, set down rules early on what will be shared emotionally, financially, and practically.

And finally – safety. Be careful about who you bring into your home. Until you are confident of someone's behaviour and intentions, they do not need to meet your child. Meet in public, take your time, and remember your role as a parent is to protect first.

The narrative that a good parent sacrifices everything is not just outdated, it is harmful. Your children benefit from seeing a happy parent.

You are not choosing your happiness over theirs, you are showing them that both can coexist. They do not need to be part of your romantic life to feel secure in your love, they need to know that whatever else changes, they remain your centre.

Part 2

Different Minds

The majority of questions we receive are about mismatches in sexual desires and different needs in relationships. These can range from mismatched libidos, body types and differing sexual desires to difficulties in satisfying a partner, judgement about one's body or sexual activities, as well as manipulation, threats and violence.

For any two people in a relationship, sexual diversity is natural. Just as in other aspects of life, we experience differences in sexual needs, and part of what makes a relationship successful is both people finding ways to navigate and resolve these differences.

Possibly the most common are questions around mismatched libidos. There can be many reasons for this mismatch. Even if you started the relationship with matching libidos, it is important to understand that this will not always be so. Libido changes as we go through life, and these changes can be brought about by age, stage of life, hormonal changes, menopause, work-related stress or relationship difficulties. In fact, not just libido but every other sexual need too is impacted by the same things.

What matters most is recognising that this is not a deal-breaker but rather a challenge that requires both partners to renegotiate and find a new path together because the shifting and changing of our sexual needs is a lifelong process – and sometimes our needs will align with our partner's, and sometimes they will not.

And in whichever direction it goes – increasing or decreasing – you must understand that this is their 'new normal'. So instead of reacting with anger or frustration and trying to bring things back to how they were or how it would suit you, the important thing here is to process what has caused the change and what adjustments may be needed to make it work for both of you. For example, is it part of a new life phase where physically they cannot be as they were before? Or could it be emotional or relational issues being expressed through sexual needs? Is it temporary, is it a desire to try something new or is it something that needs medical intervention? Each of these has a different answer.

In my experience, people will often access help for the medical aspects but struggle to get support for the emotional or relational ones, and instead of addressing these issues many end up blaming or judging their partner's sexual needs, or lack thereof.

Societal norms and stereotypes make things worse. From a young age, we are led to believe that the rules for men and women are different. That 'men have stronger sexual needs' or 'men always enjoy sex' while the 'good woman' only has sex for procreation, not pleasure, are normalised.

In relationships where women express higher sexual needs, their character is often judged. Likewise, when men experience reduced libido, they may feel it is a direct attack on their masculinity or virility. These stereotypes add unnecessary pressure and stress to an already complicated situation.

During my work in comprehensive sexuality education, I saw how harmful these stereotypes can be. Many teenagers make risky choices out of fear of being judged. For example, girls often avoid asking their partners to use condoms because they fear being seen as 'loose' or 'sexually experienced'. Afraid of ruining their reputation or losing their partner, they remain silent, putting themselves at greater risk.

Sometimes we rein in our sexual needs because of myths and stereotypes. Society often ties sexuality to morality, linking sex and sexual behaviour to character, reputation and family honour. As a result, many people make sexual choices not for fulfilment or pleasure but to protect an idealised social image that was shaped by patriarchy and an outdated morality. This is not to say that 'morality' is redundant but rather, as we have learned from history, that sexual norms are constantly shifting.

It would not be misplaced here to address pornography. In recent years, different aspects of porn have increasingly affected both individuals and relationships. Porn has always existed, so why does it seem more problematic today? The main reason is access.

Earlier, limited access to porn, available mostly via print magazines or video cassettes, meant that obtaining it required effort. Today, in the age of the internet, porn is far too accessible. And the even bigger evil is that today's porn culture is dominated by short videos that mostly focus only on the physical act. Even within the physical act, the emphasis is usually on penetrative sex rather than on foreplay, intimacy, romance or trust. Added to that, much of what is shown is digitally altered or exaggerated, making it nearly impossible to replicate in real life.

But because porn often becomes the informal 'teacher' in the absence of comprehensive sex-ed, we end up learning performance over connection and falling under the pressure to 'perform and look' like porn stars.

Porn use has also shaped people's masturbation habits, which can in turn affect their ability to have sex. Some may climax too quickly; others may struggle to orgasm without visual stimulation. This naturally creates complications in relationships. When one partner becomes reliant on porn to reach orgasm, they often cannot manage without it. Yet, because there is so little open discussion or education on the subject, this difficulty is easily misinterpreted as a lack of chemistry or interest in the partner. In reality, it is usually the result of a porn-conditioned habit – something that can be recognised and worked on. Without this understanding, however, the relationship ends up troubled.

Another growing concern is the fear of being 'addicted' to porn. Between misinformation, stigma and personal worry, anxiety around this issue too continues to rise. Once again, stereotypes play a strong role: messages such as 'women don't masturbate', 'masturbation is bad' or 'immoral people watch porn' reinforce shame. As a result, when people masturbate – especially to porn – they may believe they are immoral or 'addicted', leading them into a spiral of guilt or to seeking unnecessary rehabilitation simply because they are judging themselves through the lens of harmful stereotypes.

Honest communication is a key ingredient in building a healthy and fulfilling sexual life.

Differing sexual needs are normal, but it is honest, judgement-free communication that allows couples to turn these differences into understanding rather than conflict.

Dr Anvita Madan-Bahel

I am a 29-year-old asexual woman in a 3-year relationship with my 29-year-old partner, who is not asexual. We were open about my sexuality from the start, and he was accepting, but over time our differences have grown. While we share intimacy in other ways, I cannot handle penetration, which he would like. He has never pressured me, and I value his patience, but his needs are valid too. We want to find a way forward that respects both of us. Would sex therapy help in a situation like ours?

Historically, asexuality has been misunderstood. If someone didn't desire sex, they were often labelled celibate, weak, or frigid, depending on their gender and social expectations.

Asexuality began to be recognised as a valid sexual orientation as recently as two decades ago with the first legal acknowledgement in 2002 when New York included the term 'asexuality' in the Sexual Orientation Non-Discrimination Act. Concurrently, medical definitions were revised from the term 'hypoactive sexual desire disorder' to recognising asexuality as an identity rather than a medical condition. Society has long pushed the idea that sexual desire is essential to love and connection, making many asexual people feel they're missing a crucial piece of the puzzle. But the truth is, asexuality is just another sexual orientation, part of the vast spectrum of human experiences.

It is also important to understand that asexuality is not just about 'not liking sex'. It's a broad spectrum that can range from being 'sex-repulsed', meaning someone who may enjoy romance or touch but can feel deep discomfort around intercourse, to 'sex-favourable' asexuals who are happy to engage in sex under specific conditions, such as emotional bonding or physical curiosity or even for rare moments of sexual attraction. Just like in any other aspect of human relationships, it's nuanced and personal.

The key thing to remember is that asexuality is not about a lack of emotion or intimacy, it's about the absence of spontaneous sexual attraction. Unlike allosexual people, who feel desire towards others, asexual people may engage in sex without that internal drive, often choosing it for connection, not arousal.

You've already done something that many couples struggle with: communicated honestly from the start. And that is your strongest foundation. A good starting point is figuring out what forms of touch are comfortable for you and how much more you might be open to exploring. Sometimes, increasing emotional closeness and non-sexual physical affection, like perhaps sleeping naked together, can help a sexual partner feel more connected, even if penetration isn't always on the table.

Would you be open to engaging in sexual activities that fulfil your partner's needs without making you uncomfortable? This doesn't have to mean intercourse, it could be mutual masturbation, outercourse or other forms of sexual connection that feel safe and enjoyable for both of you. There are also different forms of sensory play, like erotic massage, temperature play, or guided touch, that can be deeply intimate and satisfying.

Or if penetration is important here, would it feel more manageable under certain conditions?

For many asexual partners, especially those who are not sex-repulsed but do not initiate sex naturally, planning sexual activity in advance can make the experience more manageable. This could be as simple as agreeing that physical intimacy happens only at certain times of the week, or only when certain rituals are followed – like having an extended emotional check-in first or doing an activity together that helps create closeness. When sex is expected to 'just happen', it can create enormous pressure, both to perform and to please. But when it's pre-agreed and approached with mutual care, it can feel safer and more grounded.

In addition to scheduling, setting clear rules can take the guesswork out of physical intimacy. For instance, you may be fine with certain kinds of touch but not others. You may be comfortable participating in your partner's pleasure in ways that don't involve your own arousal. You may want reassurance that there will be no pressure to escalate, or that a no can be said at any time without guilt. These kinds of boundaries are not restrictive, they are protective. And for the partner with a higher libido, this structure can also relieve the anxiety of constantly wondering whether they are pushing too far.

A good sex therapist or relationship counsellor can be a huge help if that resource is available to you. A sex therapist might also guide you through Sensate Focus, a technique that helps couples rediscover connection through slow, structured, non-goal-oriented touch. It's especially helpful when one partner is anxious about sex or has a complex relationship to their own arousal. This kind of therapeutic intimacy can help shift your shared focus from 'will we have sex' to 'can we feel closer in a way that suits us both'.

If, after exploring all options, no compromise feels right for both of you, some couples choose to explore ethical non-monogamy. With professional guidance, some relationships find balance by allowing the sexual partner to fulfil their needs outside the relationship with clear consent and boundaries. This is a big decision that requires deep trust and careful discussion, but for some, it can be a workable solution.

People sometimes wonder why non-monogamy would even be an issue, why would an asexual person feel jealous in a non-monogamous relationship. If they don't experience sexual desire, would it even bother them? Jealousy isn't just about sexual desire; it's tied to emotional bonds, personal insecurities, and relationship expectations. An asexual person might experience jealousy differently from a sexual person, but that doesn't mean it isn't a factor in relationships. For some, emotional intimacy is far more important than physical intimacy, so the idea of their partner forming a deep bond with someone else might be more distressing than a purely physical encounter. On the flip side, some asexual individuals experience compersion – a sense of happiness or satisfaction in seeing their partner happy, even if that happiness involves intimacy with someone else.

Either way, if you and your partner consider non-monogamy at any point please ensure you do so with professional support.

A bit of advice for the sexual partner in the relationship – understanding and respecting what your asexual partner is experiencing is essential. Asking for consent, being mindful of boundaries, and making sure your partner never feels pressured or invalidated are non-negotiables. Don't underestimate the emotional toll of feeling like your body isn't responding 'normally', even when you know you're asexual. At the end of the day, what matters most is that you and your partner both feel seen, heard, and valued in your relationship. There's no one-size-fits-all answer, but with communication, patience, and possibly professional guidance, you can work towards a solution that keeps both of you fulfilled.

What next?

Clarify your position on the asexual spectrum. Are you completely sex-repulsed or sex-favourable under specific emotional conditions? Noting your feelings before and after intimacy can also help pinpoint where your boundaries lie.

Define your personal pleasure vocabulary. Understand what kinds of touch feel good to you. This might include cuddling, certain types of massage, oral sex, mutual masturbation, or fantasy-based play. Share this with your partner and invite them to do the same.

Try structured compromise. If spontaneity is anxiety-inducing, try scheduling intimacy. Define the limits, agree on frequency, and use structure to reduce stress. Some couples use a shared calendar, others have a 'yes/no/maybe' list of activities they're willing to try.

Seek professional support. A sex therapist or relationship counsellor can guide you through this process. They can help you design intimacy that works for both of you, not as a compromise of your values, but as a deepening of your understanding.

In a long-term relationship, emotional safety is just as important as physical satisfaction. You are not failing by needing different things. You are not selfish for setting boundaries. And you are not alone in this experience. There are many couples like you learning that love is not about perfect alignment, but about respectful negotiation.

I'm a 27-year-old woman who is hitched but living with my parents. I have a partner who loves me deeply. But I'm not physically involved with him any more. We were good in the first two years, but then I lost interest, although I do get aroused by other men. I think the reason may be that the first two times we had sex, he was really rough and hit me as well because I wasn't 'cooperative' enough. Getting older and still not being able to have sex is my main concern. My gynaecologist has told me to keep trying by myself. I feel like I'll be out of the dating market soon and not be desirable to men. I worry about this a lot.

Historically and culturally, women's sexual pleasure has been treated as irrelevant, while their pain, especially when resisting male desire, has often been dismissed or even sanctioned. Patriarchal systems have positioned women as sexual objects whose primary role is to satisfy male needs, not to experience their own. Marital rape remains legally and socially accepted in many cultures, based on the belief that a wife's consent is permanent and her 'no' meaningless. A woman's no is defiance that is to be corrected, not a boundary to be respected, and if she resists, violence is not only permissible but often inevitable.

This legacy continues, and the neglect of women's pleasure and the normalisation of their pain remain deeply embedded in sexual expectations. Let's be clear, someone hitting you during sex because you weren't 'cooperative enough' is not 'love', it is not even 'rough sex', it is not a kink, it is not a moment of miscommunication – it is out and out abuse and it is a red flag the size of a building.

If someone hits you during sex because you're not doing what they want, they are not making love to you, they are using your body. This is not passion – it is power. No gift, no holiday, no 'I love you' after the fact makes it OK. That's not how love works. Love doesn't come with bruises.

Your body records and remembers the discomfort, the abuse. Even if you've convinced your brain to move past it, your body hasn't. Because your sexual organs are smart. They store memory. And if the first few experiences of sex involved pain, pressure, fear, or being shut down, your body is going to pull back every time you try to go there again. It's a survival response.

Your sexual organs are not mechanical. They don't just respond to stimulation. They respond to memory. And the body is often far more honest than the mind. It remembers things your conscious brain might want to ignore. It remembers the pain, the fear and the powerlessness. And once it's felt that, it will shut down intimacy with the person who caused it, even if the mind is still trying to hold on to the relationship.

And then, on top of all that, there's the fear that time is running out. That 27 is too old to be starting over. That you're no longer desirable. That you've missed your chance. This is a script women have been handed for generations. It's planted early and repeated often. This is not guidance. It's grooming.

And most of it comes from the people who were supposed to protect you. Parents who believe they're being practical, aunties who think they're helping, a culture that keeps telling girls they should be grateful to be chosen at all. What this really does is destroy your self-esteem so you start shrinking yourself to fit the relationship. Just like right now you are taking the blame wondering why 'you' can't focus on sex, that he is such a 'good' man there must be something wrong with you, that you are a 'slut' for thinking of other men, and so on.

But you're not 'ruining' anything. You're trying to survive something that has already crossed a line. Your body has gone into self-protection mode because it doesn't feel safe. And no, fantasising about someone else isn't a betrayal, it's your mind trying to escape. It's a coping mechanism, not a crime.

Your gynae told you to explore your own body, and she's right. Not because it's a quick fix to 'get you back on track' but because it's a way to reconnect with pleasure that belongs to you. You need to feel what safety and arousal look like without fear of 'performance pressure', to understand what turns you on when no one's watching and no one's demanding. We don't realise how deeply the body stores experiences, that it will remember touch that felt unsafe and will freeze if it senses a repeat. It doesn't mean you're broken. It means your system is working exactly as it should.

Our culture puts enormous pressure on girls to believe that being chosen by a man is the end goal. And if she hasn't been picked by a certain age, she's somehow failed. I've heard parents call it 'being realistic', but what they're doing is breaking her confidence so they can hand her off to the lowest bidder. And once that handover is complete, she's expected to be grateful, grateful for being taken and for being tolerated, for the privilege of being touched, no matter how violent that touch is. So that if the relationship starts to feel wrong she blames herself. Because that's what she's been trained to do.

To put it bluntly, you need to leave. This is not a relationship you can heal inside of. You can't stay with someone who's hurt you like this and still find a way back into your own desire. Because that would mean asking your body to forget what it knows. And your body, quite rightly, refuses.

I am a 33-year-old man and have been married for 3 years. It was an arranged marriage. My wife loves me, but she is not interested in sex, she avoids penetration and is uncomfortable with oral sex, even if she agrees to it. She prefers only hugs and kisses. I get frustrated because I have a high sex drive and had an active sex life before marriage. Sometimes I feel tempted to have an affair, but I am conflicted and feel guilty too. I have spoken to her, and she says she has low desire. Once she told me she doesn't like penises, she likes breasts, but not vaginas. It makes me wonder if she is a lesbian though she denies it. This is affecting my mood and emotional connection. I respect her, but I feel we are mismatched and I may have married the wrong person. What should I do?

Sexual attraction, especially for women, is not linear, logical or easily defined. And in arranged marriages, where many people enter the relationship without prior sexual experience or exploration, desire often doesn't happen automatically, it has to be learned, often with great difficulty. And in many cases, it can also be completely absent.

When your wife says she 'doesn't like penises', it may not be a declaration of orientation. It could be that she is uncomfortable with the idea of penetration – either because she's been taught to think of it as shameful or because of pain, or just a lack of emotional arousal in general. 'Liking breasts' doesn't make her a lesbian either, many women admire or even eroticise parts of other women's bodies without feeling sexually attracted towards them.

On the other hand, what I think she is telling you is that she's not interested in sex as she understands it or is experiencing it right now. And that's what you need to pay attention to.

Right now, you are sexually unfulfilled, while she is sexually disengaged. You specifically want penetrative sex, and that too with a willing, desiring partner, while she wants closeness, but not that kind of intimacy. There is a fundamental difference in what sex means to both of you but that's not the conversation you are having.

For some people, the absence of sexual desire isn't temporary, it may be part of their orientation. She could be asexual or sex-averse. And if that's the case, no amount of pressure, or repetitive demands will magically awaken something that isn't part of her sexual desires.

It's also important to recognise that the two of you may be speaking completely different erotic languages. You may be trying things out in the way that you know best – through physical contact, touch or other things that worked for you in your past relationships. But for her, arousal might not come from the same routes at all. Her pleasure map could be entirely different. And if something isn't working, doing it again and again will not miraculously bring different results. You may need to change the basics of what you are doing.

Then there is the all-important matter of cultural conditioning. Many women are taught to associate sex with duty and shame rather than with pleasure. In arranged marriages, especially, where there is great emphasis on being 'virginal' and 'pure' many women are thrown into the deep end with no experience or knowledge which results in them retreating from physicality altogether. So, what may look like disinterest could also stem from lack of safety, lack of education or a lifetime of emotional suppression.

The fact that she will perform oral sex for you when asked, but without enjoyment, is not a solution. That's a slow path to resentment, for both of you, because you don't want a partner who's *enduring* sex.

Which brings us to the thing you're afraid to say out loud – you're thinking of sleeping with someone else. Not because you don't care for your wife, but because your needs are not being met, and haven't been for some time. Having those feelings is not shameful, they're coming from intense frustration. But acting on them would definitely be unfair, especially if it is without trying to fix the actual problem: that you are not sexually compatible right now.

This is not an accusation, it is a simple fact – you are allowed to want more and she is allowed to have limits. The question now is what to do with that fact, because pretending that one person's needs are always on hold will not lead to a happy relationship.

I just want to add here that it is also important for you to acknowledge that you have the vocabulary to understand and articulate your needs, and it could be that she does not, perhaps it is just that she does not have the words to tell you or hasn't yet figured out what she wants. A partner who cannot, or does not, want sex isn't always because of a problem, she may just not have understood how to tell you how she would like it.

What next?
Stop asking if she's gay. That question is not helping. What matters is what kind of intimacy she wants as opposed to what kind you need. This is not about orientation but desire.

Have a real conversation. Help her figure out, in language that she understands, what level of intimacy she is looking for long term, whether she is comfortable with it or whether this is just 'how she is'.

Explore couples or sex therapy. A therapist can bring clarity and perhaps help both of you find new ways of connecting.

Rule out medical issues. There could be medical or hormonal issues that you are both unaware of, which can affect libido quite drastically. This is something often missed in conversations around desire. It is worth seeing a doctor to rule out the possibility.

If you are going to seek sex outside the marriage, do it with integrity. Redefine the relationship and mutually agree on the changes you want to make.

You don't have to stay in a marriage where intimacy has no place. But you also can't ask someone to become a version of themselves they've never been. And at this point you are the only person she has.

I am a 31-year-old single woman who sees herself as a radical feminist and a vocal advocate for women's sexual freedom. But when it comes to myself, I feel shame. I want to have sex, but I fear assault, and more than that I feel guilty about doing it outside marriage. My mother has stood by me and never judged me, but I still feel pressure to be a 'good girl' and fear disappointing her. I worry that if she found out, she would feel she failed in raising me. I also struggle with body image and intimacy, and while I support sexual freedom for others, I feel stuck in conservative ideas when it comes to myself. How do I let go of this shame?

Let me begin by saying there is nothing unusual about the way you feel. This combination of not wanting to disappoint the liberal, trusting parent who has placed their faith in you, of thinking that exploring sex and pleasure is the thing that will let them down plus the body image issues – you could be telling my story and that of countless other women.

Mothers – without meaning to – often become the keepers of inherited values. Their casual comments about 'good girls' or what they think of women who have stepped 'out of line' leave lasting emotional imprints. While we may intellectually reject those ideas, they remain in our head as trails of deeply embedded guilt.

Your mother, like many women before her, grew up with very tightly controlled rules around sex and morality, rules that were designed to 'keep her safe' in a society that saw female sexuality as dangerous unless contained. And while we now know that those rules were written in a world that did not celebrate women's pleasure or autonomy, she has passed them on, as the only way she knows, to protect you.

You wouldn't believe how many women out there feel as you do. And I'm talking about women who stand up for sexual liberation and campaign for sexual rights yet hesitate when it comes to their own desires, women who know, logically, that their worth is not tied to sexual purity but still feel uneasy about exploring their sexuality, which they have been taught to distrust.

Recently, I heard a parent say, 'We taught our daughters to be responsible for their actions, but then they do stuff that makes you think, where did I go wrong?' and it made me realise that the shame we feel around sex isn't about the act itself but about who we are when we have sex. Are we still 'good' daughters? Or, having internalised society's gaze, should we now be watched, judged and condemned?

The guilt you feel about 'breaking faith' is because we have all been taught to think of sex as a transaction – when to, who with and in return for what – and not as a natural and personal instinct of pleasure that should be based on consent, respect and emotional connection rather than marital status.

You are not betraying your mother by wanting pleasure. The values she gave you are not chains, they are starting points. Use these values to define how you explore rather than how to restrict yourself.

I also understand that part of this is our struggle with body image and intimacy. As women we treat our bodies like battlegrounds. From the start we are taught that our worth is in how we are seen, not how we feel. We are told to shrink, to soften, to be desirable but not desiring. The lens in place is 'judgement' rather than self-love. To top it all, our present level of social media interference is not helping.

Wanting sex doesn't make you immoral. I hear your fear about your consent being dismissed but this is where the true understanding of 'sexual agency' and 'values' comes into play. Sexual agency isn't about how much sex you have, it's about making informed, conscious choices that align with your comfort and desires.

The 'good girl' syndrome is not yours by nature, it is an inherited legacy but it is extremely powerful because unlike the feminist ideals that you hold, which are a conscious decision, this is embedded in the subconscious. It's difficult to place a finger on it and that makes it much harder to fight.

But fight it you must, because the shame we associate with sex doesn't just affect your sexual life, it seeps into your relationships too. Most women who write to me are so riddled with shame around sex they are not able to explore it even with their husbands. The messages we were raised with will not disappear overnight, so tell yourself that you need time to work through this.

What next?

The next time the guilt creeps in, ask yourself: who benefits from me feeling this way? Is this shame keeping me safe or is it keeping me in fear? This will help you separate your beliefs from the conditioning. When you say 'my own morality around sex really bothers me', ask yourself what morality means to you. Does it mean abstinence or conscious choices that align with your values?

Speak to your younger self. If you had a daughter, a niece, a younger version of you sitting before you, ashamed and confused, what would you tell her? Now tell yourself the same thing.

On a personal note, when I cannot untangle my thoughts I write things down. Instead of 'I am ashamed' write 'I am exploring what feels right for me' and see where that takes you.

Consider low-pressure, emotionally safe sexual experiences to explore your comfort zone. But if waiting until marriage truly feels like your choice, then honour that too. You are allowed to want or not want sex and you're allowed to take as much time as you need to decide that.

Sexual liberation isn't just about what you 'do', it's about how you 'feel' about what you do.

I run and work out at the gym regularly. I believe this could be raising my testosterone levels and increasing my libido. My girlfriend, however, has very low libido, does not enjoy sex much and rarely orgasms. This mismatch has led to several arguments. Is there a way to reduce my libido or help increase hers?

Mismatched libidos are not a modern-day issue. The *Kama Sutra* says that human beings are naturally mismatched when it comes to libidos and this is merely a hurdle to be crossed rather than an obstacle that would break the relationship. Classifying men and women into three different categories each based on their sexual appetite and arousal patterns – men are described as hares, bulls or stallions and women as deer, mares or elephants – it provides instructions on what partners can do to sync their intensity and timings. For instance, if the man is a hare (quick arousal, less stamina) and the woman an elephant (slow arousal, deep passion), he's advised to extend foreplay, focus on her pleasure, and not rush intercourse. The rule of thumb is that it is up to the partner who is more quickly aroused to adapt. And the woman's pleasure must always be prioritised and a man must practise how to delay his gratification until she is fully aroused.

Libido is never just about biology. While having an active lifestyle – running regularly, gymming, staying active – will likely elevate your testosterone levels, your libido is influenced by things other than hormones. Mental health (stress, anxiety, depression), what you eat, how much you sleep, your cultural conditioning, past traumas, body image and very importantly your relationship dynamics, meaning how safe or desired you feel, all play a significant role in how your desires manifest.

Or it could simply be a case of not understanding what gives her pleasure. Perhaps it's nothing to do with not 'wanting' it as much as you do, perhaps it simply does not feel the way she needs it to feel in order to want it.

Women's pleasure is so deeply stigmatised that most are never taught to understand what does or doesn't give them pleasure, let alone that it can be completely different from the way somebody else may want it. So this could simply be the mind creating obstacles that we don't even know about because we can't see them. So 'low libido' may not always be about not wanting sex, it may just be about not enjoying sex enough to want it again.

The stigma and silence around pleasure has created a lose-lose situation all around. For the partner with the higher libido, it can feel like rejection. You get shamed for wanting more, you get labelled 'sex obsessed' or addicts, you are left feeling that your needs are unimportant and frivolous. For the partner with the lower libido it feels like pressure. They are made to feel that they are 'abnormal' in some way, that they are the cause for the relationship falling apart and they often face veiled suggestions that their partner may need to look elsewhere for satisfaction.

Neither of these judgements is correct but each person's feelings and their perceptions of what they think is happening is valid. As the *Kama Sutra* says, libido differences are natural and we need to understand how to adapt to each other's needs rather than trying to force desire.

What next?

Change the meaning of the word sex. Sex doesn't have to mean penetration. People with lower libidos are often far more open to things like touch, oral sex, mutual masturbation, even cuddling. If penetrative intercourse is the only thing ever on the table, it can feel more like a goal-oriented activity rather than pleasure. And if sex always feels like a chore, desire dies.

Understanding her pleasure. If your girlfriend doesn't 'enjoy' sex, it's important to first work out why that is so. When you have sex (or plan for it) does she feel safe and relaxed enough to get there slowly in her own way and her own time? Or is she under pressure to feel the same arousal as you feel right away? Does she understand what gives her pleasure? Has she ever learned (or experimented with) her own arousal patterns or responses? Because unfortunately many women grow up with zero understanding of their bodies.

Does she need emotional arousal? More than just time, women's arousal often needs the right circumstances.

Spontaneous desire (the kind you may feel) is not the same as responsive desire (which many women experience). She might not feel turned on until there is a certain 'something' in place. And if that is the case her body will not signal 'yes', and the pressure of doing it will turn it into a further downward spiral.

What makes her feel sexy and confident, what makes her get to that point where she will want to initiate? You'll be surprised how much can shift when one can understand that.

You asked if there is a way you could lower your libido. I would never recommend trying to suppress your desires out of guilt or frustration. It's a natural, healthy part of who you are. So instead of lowering your desire, think about redirecting it towards something that feels good for both of you, some other kind of intimacy or sensual connection even if not sex.

Discuss between you what other ways you can enjoy connection on days when intercourse doesn't happen and ask her to take the lead on that.

And finally, as I always say, all relationships need an ongoing pact of compromise. Nothing is perfect, and even when you find a rhythm that works for both of you, that rhythm will not always be suitable.

Libido shifts with every change – time, stress, health, pregnancy, medications, emotions, etc.

And no compromise is ever fifty–fifty. Sometimes you meet in the middle, sometimes one gives a little more and sometimes it just feels like a roadblock that you have to navigate. There is no such thing as a perfect match of desire in real life – you are not wrong for wanting more, neither is she for wanting less. That's just life.

My boyfriend (22) and I (20) have been together for a year. We were both virgins when we started, and though it was difficult at first, we figured out penetrative sex. He is amazing in bed, he makes sure I orgasm every single time. But in all this time, I have never been able to make him orgasm, either through oral or penetrative sex. I've watched endless videos and tried many different techniques, but he doesn't enjoy it and doesn't even want me to do oral on him. He has only ever ejaculated when he masturbates himself and is frustrated because he wants to orgasm with a partner, and I feel so guilty I have not been able to give him that. Also, it's not a performance issue, because he stays turned on for a really long time, just doesn't orgasm in any way when I'm involved but he can easily orgasm himself.

Now he is wondering whether we should break up so he can try sex with someone else to see if it happens and I understand but it still really hurts. Is something wrong with me – am I bad at sex? I love him so much and it breaks my heart to think this could be the reason I will lose him.

I want to begin by saying, unequivocally, that only your own body can either produce or block your own orgasm. You can give someone as much pleasure, stimulation, and love as possible, but if their body is not able to respond – due to stress, hormones, medication, trauma, or countless other factors – then it will not happen. Equally, unless they are completely repulsed by you, you cannot block someone's orgasm either. That too is entirely dependent on their own body and the workings of their nervous system.

Pleasure is never that straightforward. It is fragile and unpredictable, and it can be affected by everything around us – mood, memory, habit, even a passing thought can shift everything. Being in love with, or even strongly turned on by, someone doesn't guarantee orgasm, and creating sexual compatibility often needs more than just trial and error in bed.

Unfortunately, though, we have all been conditioned to believe that male arousal in particular is mechanical – constant, emotionless, and purely visual. So if it falters in any way, as the only visible variable, the fault becomes the woman's. And so we begin endlessly scrolling through videos, rethinking every move, questioning our worth in an effort to try to fix something that is not in our power to control.

You say your boyfriend has been generous and focused on your pleasure, ensuring you orgasm each time, whereas no matter what you have tried you can never do it back for him, he can only finish through masturbation. And you are holding yourself responsible for this.

This has nothing to do with you being 'bad at sex'. What you are describing is a phenomenon known as 'partnered orgasm difficulty', and it affects more men than most people realise.

It is important to understand that masturbation and partnered sex involve completely different types of stimulation. Many men develop very specific habits around how they masturbate, not just in terms of physical rhythm, grip, pressure and angle, but also the mental comfort of privacy, the ability and control to focus entirely on their own arousal without any external pressure. Over time, both the body and mind become conditioned to respond only to that specific combination.

Partnered sex introduces two major complications. First, no matter how much stimulation is offered – whether vaginal, oral, or manual – it rarely matches the exact sensation the brain and body have become used to during solo sex. When the brain has been trained to expect a specific pattern, even pleasurable touch can feel unfamiliar or ineffective. Second, unfortunately, male sexuality is still defined by the 'action', there is immense internalised pressure to perform, and nothing shuts down orgasm faster than pressure.

This is not a dysfunction, it is simply a habit, and like any habit, it can be rewired, but you need to know that you're doing it in order to undo it.

So what should you be trying? The first step is to reframe the goal. Instead of chasing orgasm, shift the focus to pleasure. The more he fixates on whether or not he will climax, the more difficult it will become. Orgasm requires a level of surrender, both physical and psychological. And if the brain is constantly fretting about whether it will happen or not, it most likely won't.

Next, he may need to retrain his body. That means reducing the frequency of solo masturbation and using a lighter touch, a different hand, or a slower rhythm when he does. The idea is to break the link between one specific type of stimulation and orgasm. Over time, this will help the body to respond to different sensations, including those in partnered sex, which is brilliant for extending the pleasure diet.

It can also help to experiment with different positions and levels of stimulation. Some men find it easier to climax when they have more control over depth and rhythm, so try positions where he can set the pace, like him on top, or from behind.

If oral sex has not worked so far, leave it for now. Trying the same thing over and over in the hope that something will magically click is not the answer.

But also, before trying another new technique or another round of videos, have a real conversation about what sex and orgasms mean to both of you – what would pleasure look like if no one was trying to reach an end goal? This is not about 'fixing' it, it's about trying to explore each other's pleasure pathways and sensations better.

Finally, this situation needs to be approached as a shared journey, not a personal failure. It is disappointing to think that love or even effort might not be enough, but that still doesn't mean something is wrong with you. Whether this relationship lasts or not, don't let it define what you believe about yourself as a lover, because guilt has a way of cementing itself as 'fact' in our memories. And your ideas about your worth, your desirability, your ability to please, and your ability to have a successful relationship in the future will stay with you much longer than any partnership, so please make sure you take the right thoughts with you. This is not your narrative, it's just an experience.

If he is open to working on this together, that's great. But if he feels that he needs to explore sex with someone else, that is his decision to make and not a judgement on your value.

Your ability to offer pleasure, love, and connection is not limited to whether or not a man ejaculates.

My boyfriend has a problem with my previous relationship because I was emotionally connected. He too has had many hookups but he says that's not a problem because they didn't mean anything, he would be OK with mine had it been casual. I love him a lot. Please guide me on how to make him feel secure because it is up to me now.

Society has always treated women's emotional history with suspicion, while men's past hookups are at best seen as a badge of honour and at worst as harmless or irrelevant. And this double standard is reinforced by popular media, including romcoms depicting women as 'hung up on their ex' or 'carrying emotional baggage', rarely showing men being criticised for leaving behind a trail of casual encounters or having been emotionally connected with an ex. It teaches us to devalue emotional vulnerability, to see it not as strength but as instability. And your boyfriend's reaction to your past is part of this. He claims that his own history is excusable because 'it meant nothing', while yours is troubling to him because it did.

Let's start with understanding that all intimacy – emotional, physical or mental – leaves a mark. There is no such thing as an entirely 'meaningless' connection because human beings are not built that way.

Your boyfriend (perhaps unknowingly, perhaps from habituated narrative) has convinced you that you should feel ashamed of your capacity for depth, as though love and connection were liabilities. And because you have bought into this long-standing gender-biased narrative, you have willingly taken on the entire emotional labour of this relationship. You have decided that you must be the one to make him feel better, that any shortfalls on his part or future blips in the relationship are because of you, while at the same time you are not granted the right to feel upset at *his* past hookups/connections since 'they meant nothing'.

This is not the sign of an evolved partnership but in fact the worst kind of gaslighting.

What next?

The first thing is to stop apologising for your past. That you were capable of real love is not a crime. And while it is normal to feel insecure about a partner's past, you cannot carry the guilt of someone else's insecurity. It is something both parties need to work through for any partnership to grow. If you want to move forward together, you need to bring this back to a two-way conversation and call out the double standard.

Next, try to understand the real source of his insecurity, because the past may be over, but insecurity, if left unchecked, will keep poisoning the present.

Does he feel that you cannot be emotionally loyal to him because you felt that for someone else once? Many people see emotional loyalty as a one-time offering, something that, once given, cannot be given again. Or is it a fear that he is not 'good enough' in comparison? That fear is incredibly common among men, but patriarchal conditioning rarely gives them the emotional permission to speak about it.

The health of your relationship cannot rest entirely on your shoulders. You cannot carry the burden of constantly having to prove your trustworthiness or of always feeling that you are not enough. If every disagreement or breakdown circles back to your past, it will become a weapon, and blame cannot be the foundation of intimacy. He will need to shift his energy from competing with your past to investing in your future together to give the relationship a chance to succeed.

I want you to try a storytelling technique I often use in therapy. In private, write down how you remember that past relationship – what it gave you, what it meant to you, and how it ended. This process helps clarify your own thoughts and feelings; otherwise, in the middle of someone else's insecurities, their version of the story can start to take over your mind too. Right now, he is treating it like the demon, the thing that holds him back. But you know that it isn't. You need to get this very clear in your own head before you have your next conversation with him.

Ask yourself, 'If the roles were reversed, would I have blamed him in the same way?' Understanding your own emotions helps you to understand what may be making him feel unsettled and to choose the best way to communicate, whether to assert or to empathise. Stop trying to single-handedly 'fix' it for both of you and instead work on creating an emotional space together. Remind yourself that a healthy relationship is built with someone, not for someone.

My boyfriend (27) and I (31) have been dating for over a year. He says he does not feel much when we have sex. When we go for two rounds, he feels in the first round but after that the sensation reduces. He's had multiple sexual partners (25–30) in the past and he says sex was better with them. He used to say my vagina is loose, so I clench it but then he finds it difficult to enter me.

We have tried multiple positions (cowgirl, missionary; different positions like pillow under my glutes/waist, legs on his shoulder, legs around him, etc., sideways, lotus, doggy) but nothing seems to be helping him. I enjoy it but he says because of my inexperience I don't know how good it can actually feel. Now it's stuck in my head. I am continuously asking, 'Are you feeling me?', 'Are you enjoying it?', and unable to have a good time myself.

I have only had one sexual partner in the past and I dated him for 6 years. I had a good sex life with him and never had any issues. However, given my lack of experience, I do not know what the issue is now and if it is just psychological. I do not even know if his penis is small or if there is actually something wrong with my vagina. Can it be resolved? If yes, how? Do we need to consult a sexologist?

Across centuries and cultures, women's bodies have been blamed, scrutinised, and reshaped to suit male pleasure so that we still measure a woman by her 'tightness', her 'newness', and her ability to please. Words like 'loose vagina', 'ran through', and 'loss of sensation' are used as tools of control to shame, police, and make women insecure about their sexual worth.

The anthropologist Carol Vance examines how female sexuality has been managed through the regulation of 'good' and 'bad' bodies in her seminal anthology *Pleasure and Danger: Exploring Female Sexuality*. A woman who enjoys sex is already breaking one taboo; if she cannot please a man exactly the way he expects, she is made to feel defective.

There is almost no mainstream sex education that teaches men to understand their own arousal patterns or to recognise that sensation and performance can vary with context, age, emotional connection, or even the pace of stimulation. Instead, if sex is not working, we put it on the woman – she is 'too wet', 'too wide', 'too used', 'too inexperienced'. And because women are socialised to absorb that blame without question, it becomes an unceasing cycle of women trying to reshape their bodies to meet the unnatural expectations of men and men continuing to misidentify the problem from a place of judgement and ignorance.

Let's make a few things clear.

Vaginas do not get 'loose'; they are muscular, elastic structures that do not permanently stretch out from sex. And no matter how many partners someone has had, sexual experience does not give anyone the authority or the ability to define your pleasure. Saying you 'do not know what good sex feels like' simply because you have had fewer partners is not insightful. It is arrogant and condescending.

There are several reasons for your boyfriend experiencing a lack of sensation or his reduced ability to sustain multiple erections. After the first ejaculation, the penis can become less sensitive, especially if there is vigorous thrusting or prolonged stimulation. In some men, especially those accustomed to high-pressure stimulation (like a tight grip during masturbation), it can take longer for sensation to return. If he has been used to overstimulation or fast-paced sex with others, his body may have adapted to expect that level of intensity to feel aroused or reach orgasm. To repeatedly say it is because your vagina is too 'loose' or that your body does not give him tension is factually incorrect and emotionally harmful.

Alternatively, it could be what we call the refractory period, which is the time after orgasm when a person is physiologically unable to get or maintain arousal. In men, this period can last from a few minutes to several hours or even longer as they age or are under emotional stress. So if he is pushing for multiple back-to-back rounds, he may be forcing his body past its natural arousal cycle, leading to reduced sensation or even numbness.

It could also be a case of performance pressure – being anxious about how many rounds he can manage or fixated on achieving a certain 'score'. When the mind is focused on performance instead of feeling, the pressure further reduces what the body can do.

The point is there could be several reasons for his perceived lack of ability to perform as he imagines he used to – because, for now, we only have his version of events to go by – and none of these reasons have anything to do with you.

Now let's hit some realities. When someone says that by the age of 27 they have had 30 partners I think it is safe to assume that these were not meaningful sexual relationships. It is far more likely that they were a series of disconnected or brief encounters, which is not the same as emotionally or physically satisfying sex. Quantity is not quality and a high partner count does not equal wisdom or sexual skill. If anything, your ability to enjoy sex now and in the past says more about your experience than his 'scorecard' ever could.

This is not a mismatch of experience, it is a mismatch of emotional maturity. It's not your so-called lack of variety, it's that you are being made to question your adequacy at every turn.

Before you consider seeing a sexologist, you need to first deal with the long-term emotional safety of the relationship itself. If his instinct around a shared sexual concern is to blame you and undermine your confidence, then you need to fix not just the physical sensation but the trust as well. Because once trust is eroded, especially around something as vulnerable as sex, it may make the relationship more unstable.

What next?

Make it clear that you will no longer participate in conversations that frame your body as the problem. If he wants to discuss sexual satisfaction, it must include both of you, with equal emphasis on your pleasure, your comfort, and your boundaries. You are not here to audition for his approval.

Take a break from penetrative sex and instead use this time to explore what feels good for both of you, whether it is touch, fantasy, sounds, or even complete stillness. When pleasure is no longer being measured, it often finds its way back.

Work together to rethink what has been happening, not with an intent to park blame but with a real desire to make the relationship flourish. Ask whether he is willing to examine his own arousal patterns and emotional responses, and whether he can engage in this as a shared issue. If the answer is no, then you need to decide how you see your future together.

My gf and I are looking to get married but then her parents asked for my DOB. She assured me it was just for her mother's sake, who believes in horoscopes, and that it changes nothing, but now 10 astrologers have been consulted, and all 10 have said our marriage will end in disaster. Two even went as far as to say her health will be in grave danger if she goes through with it, while others declared that I will be unfaithful.

I do not understand how these charlatans can decide my character based on some horoscope, but now her parents are panicking, and my gf is panicking along with them. I don't know whether to get angry with her or laugh. I am torn and don't know what to do. I feel like shaking her to come to her senses and use science/logic – she is a doctor!

I keep sending her voice notes to cheer her up and remind her how much we love each other, but even that is burdening her now.

For now, I am giving her space to think about it. I have heard the saying that you need to let go of people and if they come back to you, they are yours, otherwise it was not meant to be.

Do you have a perspective or take on this? Would you kindly let me know?

In many South Asian families, astrology is woven into the fabric of decision-making, especially around marriage. It is not simply seen as superstition but as a form of ancestral wisdom passed down generations as a way to prevent misfortune and ensure happiness. Families turn to horoscopes not just for compatibility but for reassurance, believing that planetary alignments can determine the success or failure of a union. For many, saying no to a match because of an astrological warning is not irrational, it is responsible.

Even for those who say they don't 'believe' in it, warnings like this can still leave lingering doubts. They tend to sit in the mind and can begin to override even the strongest emotional bonds.

This is not a case of the two of you falling out of love; instead, it feels like your love is on a collision course with generational fear.

You have built a healthy, happy relationship, but it is now being held hostage by a belief that your stars are not aligned. Ten astrologers have made not vague but very specific predictions painting you as someone who will cause pain and suffering to your girlfriend. And now, the family is in full crisis mode, and worse, she is being drawn into this fear as well. Not because she does not trust you but because she has been taught that trusting her family's belief system is what keeps her safe. Even as a doctor, someone trained to look for scientific evidence, this is affecting and drowning out her own beliefs.

And this is what you find so hurtful – that if someone really loves you, how come they are not ready to fight for that love.

The problem is fear can be just as powerful as love, especially when it is dressed up as concern from people you have never been allowed to question. What your girlfriend is experiencing is not a lack of love, it is a conflict between her emotional loyalty to you and her inherited fear of 'inviting disaster' into her life.

The problem is not that astrology exists. The problem is when astrology becomes a script that overrides what a person truly knows and feels. And right now, that script is louder than your relationship.

You are right to be frustrated. The harder you try to remind her of what the two of you have built, the more it may start to feel like pressure for her and 'just not worth it any more' for you. Giving her space is the right decision, because this is not a battle you can fight any more. Now it is completely up to her to decide whether she is ready to take responsibility for her own choices.

If she can, the relationship has a real chance; if she can't, cruel as it sounds, this relationship will not stand the test of time. Because life will always bring challenges, and if every difficulty makes her wonder whether the astrologers were right after all, the relationship will eventually collapse under the weight of that doubt.

You are right, you cannot force her to return, but you cannot let this define you either. You are not unworthy, you are not a villain, and you are not the person the 10 astrologers are talking about.

What you feel for her is honest and real; it is up to her to decide whether or not this is enough for her. If she does not come back, the heartbreak will be real, and you're absolutely allowed to feel the hurt. But you cannot let that define the 'you' of tomorrow.

What next?

Step back and give her some space, not to test her but to allow her to come to her own decision without panic or pressure. She must choose this relationship freely if it is to survive.

Separate the fear from the person. Understand that her withdrawal is not about a lack of love but about being overwhelmed by the authority of her parents and the generational weight of the system. Do not take it personally, but don't feel like you have to pretend it is not hurting either.

Protect your emotional energy. You cannot fight 10 astrologers, two panicked parents, and her uncertainty all at once. You can only hold your own ground. Do not let the need to 'keep her close' drain you of your own peace.

My husband loves me but when it comes to sex he just watches porn and masturbates because he says it is easier and less work. He says we can share everything else, everything emotional, but not this. I am confused and wonder if it is because he isn't attracted to me. How can a relationship survive like this? I want sex, what can I do?

Watching porn or masturbating is not in itself the problem. In fact, solo pleasure is a very important part of our sexual wellness and there is nothing wrong with using porn as one of the tools for self-pleasure, as long as it is occasional, consensual and does not replace shared intimacy.

The problem arises when someone decides to entirely replace sex with porn because that means you emotionally and physically disconnect from the relationship.

Porn is attractive because, unlike partnered sex, which can be messy, unpredictable and hard work, it is fast, controlled and guaranteed – no performance anxiety, no negotiation, no explanations, just 'reliable' and instant.

But this is also what makes it problematic, because there is no need for consent or boundaries or what your partner wants or if something hurts them – basically, you lose any sense of responsibility towards another person's body or feelings. And over time, this becomes your wiring – you don't just detach from your partner, you forget how to be a partner. Because when you get used to sex being about taking what you want without conversation, you begin to expect that in the real world too. And that is dangerous. And for the person living with this, it can be seriously damaging. When you see your partner consciously choosing an alternative source of pleasure over you every time, it can destroy your self-esteem and have you questioning your worth.

This is not healthy at any level. So what can you do?

As always, we need to begin with a conversation, but the conversation needs to be about the relationship, not porn. It may be difficult to separate the two, given the circumstances, but it's important to remember you are not there to argue about whether porn is 'right' or 'wrong'. That will get you nowhere. Frame it as a question about connection. Tell him clearly that you need the physical side of things as well to stay in the relationship and how his behaviour is making you feel.

If he is ready to talk, tell him you are happy to support him too – what is the first step he needs help with, what is it about partnered sex that feels like effort, what are the most important things that porn gives him that intimacy does not, and what can you do together to make it feel less like effort and more like pleasure?

Don't be apologetic about your needs. Remind yourself that you are not being unreasonable by wanting sexual connection in the relationship. Intimacy is not a bonus – it is part of the basic structure. If he wants emotional closeness but not physical closeness, and that too because he would, in essence, rather do that 'with someone else', he is offering you only half a relationship, and you need to decide if you're OK with that.

If nothing changes, could ethical non-monogamy be a viable option for you? This is not about punishing him or 'shocking' him into doing what you want, but if you want to stay in the relationship and still meet your sexual needs and he absolutely refuses to compromise, this is one of the few choices available to you. It will not rebuild your connection, but it might allow you to stay without feeling entirely deprived. This may not be a path you are willing to take at all, in which case you have some serious decisions to make. Because remaining in a sexually disconnected relationship out of fear or confusion will slowly drain your sense of worth.

Do not internalise this. This is not a sign that you are unattractive or not good enough. He is just choosing to fulfil himself without wanting to put any 'work' into it. And if he continues to do this without taking your needs into consideration, that is a whole different level of entitlement.

We are conditioned to apologise for our own needs, to accept less while being grateful for the 'love' we are given – no matter how lacking it might be. The real question is – what kind of relationship do you want to be in? And is this one offering that? In the end only you can decide that.

What exactly is porn addiction? I like porn and sometimes I watch just to fill the gap in the day and sometimes to feel better about sex. Sometimes after porn we end up having amazing sex but sometimes it makes me not want it with my partner; it feels less exciting. Is this addiction? Is it harmful? How can I stop?

'Addiction' is when a behaviour starts to interfere with your life, when it stops you from being able to go about your daily work, gets in the way of your well-being and relationships, yet you cannot control or stop it.

Porn habits can fall along a wide spectrum from watching occasionally out of curiosity or boredom to using it to enhance solo or even partnered pleasure to relying on it daily to cope with stress, loneliness or lack of physical intimacy. There is nothing inherently wrong with watching porn. But when it becomes the primary and only way someone engages with sexual pleasure, it can completely redefine how they look at arousal, relationships, bodies and even sex itself.

The problem is not just about what you are watching but about what it replaces. Porn is fast, convenient and hyper-stimulating because it can offer you any fantasy without any kind of effort. In return, it demands nothing from you – no communication, no presence, no caring, literally no work – all of which are essential in real-life intimacy. Over time, overuse of porn can make partnered sex feel less exciting because it dulls your own imagination so that you cannot get aroused without the stories that it is providing, but even more it destroys your ability to focus during sex because of the effort that needs. And that can seriously affect your relationship.

If you or your partner are in a situation where porn has taken over your life, here are a few tips to start shifting that habit.

1. Don't start with 'never again'.
   Going from 100 to 0 abruptly and completely often results in guilt, secrecy or binge behaviour. Start by choosing specific times or days to avoid porn entirely. For example, decide not to use porn before bed or during work breaks. Slowly reduce the frequency and notice how your mind and body respond. The goal is to become aware of the impulses, not to punish yourself.
2. Identify your triggers.
   Most people do not watch porn just for the orgasm. It is often a response to something else – stress, anxiety, boredom, rejection, loneliness. Track what happened right before. How were you feeling? What felt easier when you finished? Once you know what your triggers are it's easier to reach for alternatives, which could be as simple as taking a walk, calling a friend, exercising or simply acknowledging the feeling and riding it out.
3. Replace with something else that feels good.
   Porn offers a dopamine hit. If you want to change the habit, you have to find alternative activities that also release feel-good hormones. That could be a workout, a dance class, cooking or even just reading erotica, which allows you to build arousal more slowly and deliberately than the instant imagery that porn offers. The body and brain are flexible, but they need help to rewire.
4. Rethink masturbation.
   Masturbation without porn is a different experience. It is slower and more introspective. It might be harder at first because you are used to being visually stimulated instantly, but it allows you to understand your own arousal more deeply and that can help you rewire your pleasure pathways.
5. Do not expect partnered sex to be like porn.
   One of the biggest problems with porn is that you start believing all those bodies, positions, noises, orgasms and

responses are real. Real sex is very unlike what you see onscreen. So if you catch yourself mentally comparing your partner to what you have seen online, pause and consciously remind yourself that porn is a scripted performance, not real human interaction.
6. Talk about it with someone.
Not necessarily a therapist, but someone you trust who will not shame you. Saying it out loud – 'I think I rely too much on porn and I'm trying to stop' – can shift the pressure that you are starting to feel. If you do want more structured help, there are sex therapists who specialise in this exact issue. It is more common than you think, and there is no shame in seeking support.
7. Curate your environment.
Your phone and laptop are not just tools, they are temptation machines. Use screen timers, get rid of shortcuts, unsubscribe from platforms that are flooding you with adult content (even if temporarily) and block triggering sites. You do not need to shame yourself for watching, but you can reduce how easy you make it for yourself. Make access a little more intentional instead of automatic.
8. Understand your reasons.
Why do you want to stop watching porn? Do you want to feel more connected with your partner? Do you want to rebuild interest in real sex? Do you want to feel more in control of your time and emotions? Get clear on the reason, because this is what will carry you through the moments when it feels difficult. Porn is not the enemy. The goal is to make it a choice not a compulsion.
9. Be realistic about relapses.
There will be days when you go back to it – that doesn't mean you failed. We are human, we can and do slip up. The key is not to spiral into guilt or give up. Just take a deep breath and start again. Every time you manage to

interrupt the pattern, you retrain your mind a little bit more.
10. Rebuild your erotic imagination.

Porn simplifies arousal into a visual transaction. But real pleasure comes from engaging all the senses. Read erotic literature, fantasise with detail, explore touch and sensation at a slower pace. The more your mind can engage with desire in imaginative ways, the more you enjoy the fact that it can take longer.

This is not about moral policing, it is about having the freedom to choose how you want to engage with your own arousal.

Porn is not part of your body, it can sometimes become your default setting, and you can reset it.

My boyfriend and I were together for 3 years and had a great sex life. We have just moved in together and suddenly he doesn't want sex any more. Doesn't even feel like it. Does he not love me any more? Am I a mistake?

When faced with disconnect and silence, most of us tend to assume that it 'must be me', that a drop in sexual interest means love has faded or that something is wrong with you. But it is not always about losing desire or getting bored. More often, it is what sex itself means to us that shifts.

When you're dating, sex feels carefree, where the only focus is pleasure. Once the relationship becomes committed, sex starts to carry more emotional weight. The relationship now has to carry the weight of a shared future, and sex becomes the symbol of that long-term compatibility – of closeness and trust and a deeper connection.

The contradiction is that we are told emotional connection should matter more than sex, that true intimacy lies in conversation, care and shared goals. But at the same time, sex becomes the silent benchmark expected to reflect how strong the bond is, how connected you are and how much you continue to desire each other. We are told that sex is no longer central while being expected to sustain it and keep it constantly fresh and ever evolving as proof that the relationship is thriving. And so what once felt spontaneous now feels burdened with emotional expectations, leading partners to overthink, and for many this subtle shift can turn sex from pleasure to pressure.

Add to that the shifting power dynamics – stepping into relationship labels like 'husband' or 'wife' can consciously or unconsciously alter how you behave in bed. Subconscious fears around autonomy may arise. The idea of being with one person forever can feel stifling, even if the emotional bond remains strong. For some the attachment styles play a role – those with anxious attachment may seek more sex for reassurance, while avoidant partners may pull away altogether, to manage their discomfort with closeness.

Sometimes, desire also dips due to stress, fatigue, anxiety or unspoken resentment, all of which are common during life transitions like moving in together.

Each of these patterns, conscious or otherwise, can unwittingly reshape how we feel and express desire as the relationship deepens.

Moving in means new routines, less privacy, more exposure to each other's habits. What was once romantic or charged can become ordinary. That adjustment phase can flatten arousal temporarily.

So how do we fix this?

This is not about lost desire, it is a shift in how you feel it. Arguing or demanding is not going to push it back into its slot, but neither will pretending there isn't a problem fix the issue. This needs work.

Sex is not a separate compartment in a relationship. When that connection breaks down, it very quickly starts affecting how you talk to each other, how you feel, even your readiness to fix the problems that crop up between you. Which is why ignoring it is not an option.

The first step is to talk about it. Most partners are left in the dark, wondering whether the relationship is falling apart and agonising over whether they were somehow to blame, which is very unfair.

If you are the one whose desire has changed, you need to be honest. You may not want sex right now and that is valid, but you need to acknowledge that the shift is affecting them as well – you owe your partner reassurance and effort.

Equally, if you are the partner feeling rejected, it is important to listen without dismissing or belittling the other's experience or becoming defensive. It is easy to shut down when you feel unwanted; treating your partner's discomfort like a personal insult only deepens the rift.

Once both of you feel safe enough to talk, begin to ask why this is happening. Is it stress, fear, resentment, routine? What are the changes that feel subtly threatening? Has sex started to feel like an obligation or test to prove closeness rather than something you simply enjoy?

Then start to rebuild physical closeness without making it all about sex, activities that can be physical but not sexual. The goal is to explore intimacy without pressure of performing.

And finally, check how you are communicating outside the bedroom. If there is resentment, criticism or tension in daily life, it will show up in your sex life.

Many couples experience a dip in sexual frequency after major transitions, so it is not uncommon, but if your partner continues in this pattern and is not willing to either talk or try, you should get professional help from someone who understands how to navigate this because it can easily become a long-term dynamic that is not easy to reverse.

If the relationship matters, then so does this.

I'm recently married and me and my partner are very much happy with our physical and mental relationship. But the thing is when it comes to physical, I really find her very cute or I can say I see her as a small kid so I can't initiate the session unless it becomes something else. So I'm basically stuck at the initial stage where I cannot start even though it's my wife. I really love her a lot but I don't want this perception to affect my physical relationship. Any suggestions how I can overcome this situation.

Emotional love and erotic desire operate through different triggers.

Among the myriad destructive stereotypes around sex and pleasure that we have inherited one of the most damaging is the idea that sexual desire must be categorised as either 'lust' or 'love'. We are taught that desire is just something that exists within us, waiting to jump up, and, especially for men, does not need to be nurtured or developed.

Further, we are told that feeling aroused by someone outside a societally approved relationship is lust – it is immoral and to be extinguished. But for a spouse (approved by the relationship system) that same desire becomes a moral obligation and, now rebranded as 'love', it is expected to appear on command, regardless of what actually turns you on.

Commitment does not guarantee arousal. A deep emotional connection is essential for intimacy, but when expressed only through comfort and familiarity, it can often flatten sexual charge. Sexual desire needs some kind of tension or mystery – perhaps glimpses of your partner that feel new, bold or slightly out of reach, slightly unpredictable rather than comfortable.

This is why we emphasise the importance of understanding how to actively build the spark, because nothing is automatic.

Building erotic desire is not about 'more intimacy', but a different kind of intimacy.

You describe your wife as 'very cute', almost childlike, and this blocks arousal. This is not about your love for her, it is your brain interpreting those specific behaviours as non-erotic.

You would not believe how many couples face this exact issue. Unfortunately, women are constantly being taught – by media, romance columns, social conditioning – that men prefer 'delicate and dependent' because it makes them feel more masculine. 'Sweetness' is rewarded with praise and approval while assertiveness is 'penalised', even by the men themselves. Hence many women learn to 'perform cutesy' as a marker of desirability. The belief is that being 'adorable' or 'vulnerable' will make him love you more.

But feeling protective is not the same as feeling aroused and the mind creates these boundaries instinctively.

And this is not just a 'woman' problem. The same stereotype also tells men that to feel masculine, they must be protectors, that physical strength is the foundation of manhood. They are never taught to articulate what turns them on, their arousal is supposed to be on tap. Being able to provide stability and support definitely creates the core of love between couples, but for a lot of men, being placed in the role of constant protector slowly dulls sexual desire. Erotic charge, ironically, needs a sense of equality.

For most men, it is the independent, witty, confident woman, the 'disapproved of' one, who triggers arousal.

What next?

I am glad you have brought this up, most people never realise it consciously, and the fact that you have done so before it turns into frustration or withdrawal shows emotional maturity. Erotic energy is not a rigid platform, it is co-created between partners. You can shift the tone of your relationship by adjusting small rituals.

My favourite is the jewellery ritual. Ask her to wear a single piece of jewellery she normally would not wear at home, perhaps anklets, a thin waistband, or a long chain down the back. This is not for decoration, it is about creating a small shift in how the body feels and moves. When she walks, sits, or turns, the ornament draws awareness to different parts of the body in different ways, to signal a shift.

Another powerful ritual is occasionally being part of her getting dressed. No sexual touch, just slow, attentive gestures of perhaps brushing her hair or adjusting her clothes while she watches herself in the mirror. It allows her to see herself through your gaze, not as someone cute or childlike, but as a grown woman being seen with quiet intent.

Create space for other facets of her personality to emerge. Most women carry within them confidence, boldness, assertiveness and a playfulness that is sensual rather than sweet. These small shifts help tell the nervous system that the energy has changed, that this is a different kind of intimacy.

Pay attention to when arousal begins, what helps it grow, and what shuts it down. Once you know those patterns, it becomes easier to go forward.

Communicate. But when you speak with her, avoid using the word 'childlike'. Instead, describe the specific behaviours that you find hard to respond to sexually. The goal is not to criticise, but to help each other understand the difference between romantic comfort and erotic responsiveness. Ask her what does or doesn't work for her so it can be a shared conversation.

Part 3
Navigating Queerness

The word 'Queer' is often used as an umbrella term for sexual orientations or gender identities that do not conform to heteronormative or cisgender norms. Put simply, it covers the wide range of desires, fantasies and identities that fall outside the heterosexual box.

Most people, at some point or other, have experienced moments of same-sex attraction, whether flirting, fantasising or experimenting. Often, these experiences are enjoyable, but they can lead to confusion because society insists that every action must fit into a fixed label.

We live in a culture where heterosexuality is treated as the norm, while same-sex intimacy is surrounded by stigma and misinformation. This leaves many people worried about what their desires 'mean'. Yet queer experience is neither an exception nor is it abnormal.

The Kinsey scale illustrates this spectrum by placing sexuality on a continuum rather than a strict binary of heterosexual or homosexual. Thinking of sexuality as fluid, like a river that shifts and flows, it not only offers choice but also the freedom to change over time.

Fear often arises from the belief that sexuality must be static. Someone may fantasise about a same-sex friend or find pleasure in experimenting, but immediately feel pressured to redefine their entire identity. In a society still shaped by homophobia, even fleeting curiosity can cause panic, turning exploration into a source of guilt.

Seeing sexuality as fluid removes this burden. For some, same-sex intimacy may be an occasional source of pleasure without altering identity. For others, it may signal a deeper recognition of themselves as bisexual, gay or lesbian. Both experiences are valid.

For instance, there is the recently widowed man who finds himself unable to be with another woman because it disrupts his memory of his wife and so he ends up going to queer male sex workers to satisfy his physical needs. Not because he identifies as gay, but because it allows him to experience release without threatening his memory of his marriage. Another man, involved in a threesome with his wife and another man, finds himself unexpectedly aroused by the other man, seeing him through his wife's eyes and feeling pleasure by imagining her pleasure. Neither man 'identifies as gay or has become gay', they have just discovered that desire is not always linear.

History is full of stories of same-sex intimacy practised simply as a source of pleasure, separate from identity or politics. It is accepted that a person could enjoy same-sex intimacy while identifying as a heterosexual – these desires are neither new nor unnatural. Yet for many of us, these same-sex desires, which should bring joy, often cause stress. Many people panic that a single fantasy or experiment defines them forever.

Exploring the question 'Am I gay?' is rarely straightforward. Researchers believe that most people fall somewhere along a continuum of bisexuality, with very few at the absolute extremes of being exclusively homosexual or exclusively heterosexual. Fantasising about someone of the same sex, or even acting on that attraction, does not automatically define a person's orientation. You may have a same-sex experience and not identify as gay, lesbian or bisexual, or you may have the same experience and choose to adopt one of those identities. The point is not the label but the acceptance of sexual diversity. What makes this difficult is the weight of homophobia – not only in the world around us but also within ourselves. Many of us grow up internalising messages that same-sex desire is shameful or 'unnatural', and these beliefs can shape the way we see ourselves long before we even begin to explore attraction.

Self-acceptance becomes even harder because society provides little support for alternative narratives. There is often no education about LGBTQ relationships, no role models who show what these lives can look like and few spaces where young people feel safe to ask questions. Without this foundation, the fear of rejection by family, friends or community can be overwhelming, reinforcing the idea that difference must be hidden. Overcoming internalised homophobia therefore requires unlearning years of stigma and replacing it with compassion for ourselves. And even when that step is taken, the work does not end: for many people, living openly means a lifelong process of 'coming out' again and again, each time hoping that others will respond with acceptance rather than hostility.

Fantasising about or engaging with someone of the same sex, and enjoying it, does not automatically determine identity. You may engage in sexual activity with a same-sex partner purely for pleasure, or it may mark the beginning of realising that you are bisexual, gay or lesbian. Both are legitimate.

To conclude, I would like to reiterate that 'Queer' experience is simply part of being human. Allow yourself to explore your sexual needs without guilt or pressure to fit into boxes.

Dr Anvita Madan-Bahel

I am a 27-year-old bisexual man, in love with another bi-man. We lived together for a year like an unofficially married couple. But now my partner is being forced by his family to marry a girl, and he has agreed. He says he will take care of me even after his marriage, that whoever comes into his life would be a wife to both of us. And later he suggested that I also marry a girl so that we can both come out to them and after a few years we four will be happy together.

Can this even work, Ma'am? I'm so scared and depressed.

Even though the term 'bisexual' as an identity is relatively recent, people have been attracted to more than one gender throughout recorded history. There has always been some recognition, though not always widespread, that sexuality exists on a spectrum, and that people may shift along it over time.

Being bisexual means having the capacity to be attracted to more than one gender. This does not mean an equal attraction to men and women, or even at the same time. Many bisexual people prefer one gender over another, and that preference may shift over time. Some may feel strong physical attraction to one gender but deep emotional connection to another. Everyone is different. But society often flattens that nuance, assuming bisexual people are either gay or straight, depending on who they are dating.

Unfortunately, stigma against bisexuality persists, sometimes even more intensely than for gay or lesbian individuals. The shifting nature of attraction is often viewed as confusion or indecisiveness, and the capacity to love more than one gender is often misunderstood as promiscuity.

Non-heterosexual relationships have always existed but have rarely been given social legitimacy. Even today, in many communities the family unit is built around heterosexual ties, with same-sex love expected to remain private and silent.

As a result, many queer people are pressured into marrying someone of the opposite sex to maintain social appearances.

When I first read this question, my immediate concern wasn't about the challenges you are facing as a bisexual individual but about the disturbingly casual dismissal of consent for the two unknown women who might enter your and your partner's lives. (For reference, the dictionary defines 'consent' as agreeing to an action based on the knowledge of what that action involves, its likely consequences and having the option of saying no.)

Here it isn't just a case of misinterpreting no as yes – it's about denying these two unknown women even the most basic right to make a decision, which to me is the worst kind of objectification. You have reduced them from human beings with thoughts and needs to 'blinds' to help you maintain appearances, as though women are just collateral damage in your personal struggle with identity and societal pressure.

Did your partner believe they would happily agree to this arrangement, that they did not deserve to know what kind of marriage they were being made to get into? This is not just ethically problematic, it is deeply unfair. The stigma attached to bisexuality can make life extremely challenging, but that cannot justify deceiving others or ignoring their agency. Queerness is not a licence to override consent.

Now as to your question on whether relationships like this work – broadly speaking, such relationships are extremely difficult to sustain. What might begin with secrecy and compromise often becomes exhausting. It takes immense courage to resist family, tradition, and social expectations, and from what you have described, your partner does not seem willing to take that step even now. If he cannot be honest today, it is unlikely that he will be more honest or more committed later.

There is nothing wrong with being bisexual, and nothing wrong with loving a man who is also struggling to find his place in the world. But if his plan for your future depends on lies, silence and collateral damage, then it is not a future worth investing in.

What next?
Do not build your emotional future around someone else's indecision. If he cannot be honest with his family now, it is unlikely that he will be in the future. You need to find your own clarity. You cannot lose yourself, trying to hold on to someone who is not fully with you. This may have been love, but if it is now damaging your mental health, it no longer is. If the only way this plan works is through secrecy or denial or by deceiving others, it is not a plan that deserves your energy.

There is life beyond this relationship. Find people, online or in person, who understand your fears and your identity and build your community and safe space around them.

I want to add a note here to all parents – the 'what will people say' mindset is just a trap. In the end, the only ones who truly win are those who prioritise what's best for themselves and their loved ones, rather than worrying about what others think.

I'm a 24-year-old straight woman dating a 35-year-old man who is married but in an open relationship. I knew he liked to cross-dress, and at first I was OK with it, but now I'm finding it harder to accept him in women's clothing. He also has a name for his female persona. I still like him when he's presenting as a man – we have intense, pleasurable sex – but I'm feeling confused and conflicted. I can't leave him just because of this. What do I do?

Cross-dressing often gets misinterpreted as a sexual kink, a sign of homosexuality, or an identity crisis. But the reality is far more layered. Cross-dressing is not new, and it is not unnatural. Stories from across cultures and eras have depicted gender transformation – not always as rebellion, but often as a form of survival, strategy, or emotional truth. From Arjuna living as Brihannala to meet the conditions of exile, Achilles disguised as Pyrrha to avoid the Trojan war, Kit Cavanaugh dressed as a man to join the army – history and mythology abound with examples of cross-dressing. But while female-to-male cross-dressing has historically been linked to courage or necessity, men in feminine clothing continue to be mocked or pathologised. As Billy Porter famously said, 'A woman in a suit is powerful. A man in a dress is a punchline.' That cultural double standard affects not just the man who cross-dresses but also the partner trying to support him.

You are not wrong for feeling disoriented. If this started as an attraction to a man and that's where your desires lie, then watching your partner present himself as a woman, complete with a name and persona, can feel like you are losing the person you love. Attraction is not just about emotional connection, it is also about how a person looks, smells, moves, and dresses. If that visual changes, it is entirely possible, nay likely, that your body may not respond in the same way. This does not make you shallow, it's simply our inner reality.

But no matter how uncomfortable this makes you feel, you need to understand that this side of him is not going to disappear. If he has named his female persona, if he cross-dresses regularly, and if he has introduced this identity into your relationship, this is not a passing phase. And even if he claims this is only for certain moods or private moments, there is every chance it will evolve into more. Not because he's lying, but because many people who explore gender fluidity do so in stages. What starts as lingerie in private may become dresses at home, then makeup in public, etc. You cannot stop this journey, and he cannot rewind it, so the only way forward is through clear, honest communication.

For instance, I have seen people get very anxious about their cross-dressing partner's online activities, the fear being that they are looking for sex, specifically with someone who may feel more attracted to them in their female-presenting persona. While that may sometimes be the case, more often than not they are just looking for practical information like where to buy clothes that fit, how to do makeup on male features, how to walk in heels, etc. Things most women take for granted but men have to learn from scratch; and generally, like-minded people online are the only ones they can reach out to.

This is where communication is all-important – because the problem isn't what he's doing online, it's what your mind imagines he's doing. You need to talk to him about it, be part of what he is looking at, diminish the mystery.

It is also normal to worry about what this means for his sexuality. Cross-dressing does not automatically imply same-sex attraction. Many men who cross-dress are heterosexual in their male identity, but their desires may shift slightly when they present in their feminine form. He's not trying to deceive you, but it is complex and can be very hard on partners; pretending it is straightforward or temporary is not going to help.

And that brings me to possibly the most important piece of advice for you – get a support network in place for yourself. It is completely understandable that you are unsure about your boundaries, or that you are worried about what people may say, or even that you feel ashamed for feeling uncomfortable. That he is older and married and gender-non-conforming probably already makes it difficult to be open about this relationship, and I don't want you to add more pressure to your life, but you need to start being honest with yourself because, beyond emotions and doubts, there are very real everyday logistics to deal with.

Will he dress this way around your friends? What if family visits? Can you deal with gossiping neighbours and domestic help? The discomfort is real.

Finally, a small but essential point on ground reality. For many people there is no distinction between cross-dressing, trans or gay, and there is no legally enforceable protection for cross-dressing – which means you're navigating both personal uncertainty and public ignorance. A major reason for the internal conflict you are facing may be the culture we're surrounded by.

What next?

Have a clear conversation about physical and emotional boundaries. Talk about where he may wish to dress this way and where and when you feel comfortable seeing it – in the bedroom, at home, in public – and whether you can both agree on this.

Give yourself permission to feel confused. Just because you love someone does not mean you automatically understand or accept every part of them. You are allowed to be uncertain, to take time to draw a line. Maybe you'll find that your attraction grows. Maybe it won't. But don't lock yourself into one idea of who he is or who you are.

Check in with your own emotional bandwidth. Supporting a partner through gender exploration is not a neutral process. It will demand energy, resilience, and self-reflection. If you begin to feel you are losing yourself in the process, pause and seek help, for your sake, and for the health of the relationship.

This isn't about choosing between 'accepting him or losing him'. This is about building a relationship that makes you both comfortable. If you're constantly suppressing your discomfort just to make the relationship work, it will crack. And building a relationship starts with honesty, not just with him, but with yourself.

I am a heterosexual man, attracted to the female body, with no arousal whatsoever from male bodies. In fact, I feel slightly repulsed if a man's touch lingers too long on my back or arm. But in my thirties, I began feeling intensely aroused by transwomen, meaning individuals who look fully like women but still have a functioning penis. My fantasies often placed me in the 'bottom' role, which made me uncomfortable.

Eventually, because the fantasy began occupying my mind too much, I visited a sex worker for two sessions, with full medical precautions. The first time was awkward, I was nervous, and nothing much happened aside from immediate premature ejaculation when she touched me. The second time, I was more composed. I told her I wanted to kiss her, perform oral sex on her, and have her top me. The entire experience was deeply arousing. I was surprised by how much I enjoyed the sensation of her penis in my mouth, and when she penetrated me, the sense of surrender was overwhelming. I could only respond – it felt like she was completely in control.

Afterwards, I felt alert and refreshed, not drained like I usually do after sex with a woman. In fact, I felt I had briefly experienced something like the pleasure women must feel during sex with a man, although this could just be my unfounded and biased reaction.

Now I feel confused. I would not mind repeating the experience, though I probably will not, due to my personal situation. But the old anxieties have resurfaced, social fears about what this means, and whether it suggests I am secretly gay. Yet my attraction to women remains completely intact.

How should I understand this, and how do I move forward?

Let us begin with some fundamental points.

Sexuality is far more layered and fluid than we have been led to believe. Pleasure can come in many different shapes, all of which are valid. But neither does one experience override the rest of who you are.

I am not here to tell you whether you are straight, bi or even bi-curious because your arousal or curiosity do not need to fit into a single, rigid identity label. This encounter has expanded your understanding of what desire can feel like in your body and that's an awareness that many people never experience.

Attraction to femininity can take many shapes because femininity itself is not just a biological checklist, it's a felt experience. Whether it is how someone looks or how they behave or their emotional intelligence, whether it is the soft, nurturing aspect or the flirtatious sensuality and emotional intelligence, it can be embodied in countless forms, and what you responded to was a version of femininity that your body recognised and desired. The presence of a penis does not cancel out those qualities. All it does is complicate the script around sexual identity, desire and femininity that we have been taught.

So let's for a while put aside preconceptions and focus instead on the arousal and sensations that you felt.

What you are describing is a shift in sexual dynamics, specifically the desire to receive or 'bottom', which many heterosexual men are socially discouraged from exploring. We've been taught to believe that 'being penetrated' is feminine or even 'lesser', while masculinity means to 'control'.

But as the *Kama Sutra* says, positions don't have gender, they create sensations. So by shifting roles we access different types of arousal and release, and surrendering control, especially for someone usually in the dominant role, can create a profound psychological and physical intensity by allowing you to access something that we are rarely permitted to experience.

Erotic fantasies often contain elements or scenarios of transgression, even contradictions that would never play out in their real-life relationships. Your attraction to transwomen, and even your enjoyment of being in a different sexual role, is not a threat, it is part of the landscape of erotic imagination, and you are allowed to explore that without needing to reclassify yourself.

That said, it is understandable that the experience brought up discomfort. These feelings are often less about the act itself and more about what we have been taught. From an early age, many men are conditioned to equate same-sex contact with guilt, shame or the erosion of masculinity. In cultures where homosexuality is stigmatised, even fleeting curiosity can feel like a threat to identity. And when an experience delivers a kind of pleasure that was unexpected in spite of being socially discouraged, it can trigger deep-seated fears. Your anxiety is not a flaw, it is a by-product of a culture that is still learning how to make space for sexual complexity.

You also mention that after being penetrated you felt that you had experienced something of what women must feel during sex. That is a powerful realisation, and one that deserves careful unpacking. Penetration alone does not equate to the female sexual experience, and we must be cautious not to reduce 'what it feels like to be a woman' to that physical act. But what you may have tapped into is the psychological experience often associated with feminine-coded sexual roles which are surrender, vulnerability and the pleasure of receiving without pressure. You found that transformative, and the honesty with which you expressed that pleasure, even while it challenges your usual understanding of pleasure, is what you should hold on to, not the socially instilled guilt.

The experience was safe and consensual, you listened to your body, you made a deliberate choice, you ensured safety and respect, and you came away feeling more alert and in tune with yourself. This is not confusion, this is emotional and sexual maturity.

It is also entirely valid not to wish to repeat it. Whether it's because it doesn't align with your life right now or whether the emotional ambiguity it introduces is too difficult to carry, it is entirely your decision. Just don't let it be because of shame. Choosing not to repeat something because it no longer feels right is different from thinking you're doing 'wrong'.

Understanding what aroused you in that moment is not about identity but about developing greater sexual self-awareness.

What might be useful at this point is not to pretend it never happened but to reflect on where that pleasure came from. Was it about surrender, was it about pleasure without pressure, was it about being touched or seen in a way that bypassed your usual mental blocks or was it just about novelty? Intensely pleasurable sex is an extraordinarily powerful way to understand our emotional depths which normally never get explored. The goal is not to label the experience but to become aware of what it reveals about your desires, so that future choices are guided by insight, not impulse.

I'm a pre-op trans, I met a guy on a dating app, we hung out every day for 5 months like couples, going out, meeting each other's friends, etc. He even introduced me to his siblings.

We'd have sex almost every day and he would say how much he likes me and misses me when I'm not around. I found myself getting emotionally attached to him. But I found out that at the same time he was still having phone sex with his ex because she lives out of town.

Then one day he sends me a text saying he wants to end it as he wants to have a wife who can give him kids. He kept saying how amazing I am and no one could ever give him a bj like me but he needs to cut off all ties till things have settled and then have a platonic friendship with me.

Post breaking up with me, we met twice where he kept insisting on being platonic but we ended up having sex each time. But when I was leaving he said the same thing, that we can't meet and this can't go on.

Am I the problem in all of this, I can't seem to forgive myself. Do you think he was never into me and just wanted me around because the sex was good? I'm so confused, cause I did not do anything wrong the whole relationship. Also, he didn't wanna put a label but when he broke up with me, he kept saying I was an amazing girlfriend and it was one of the best relationships he'd been in. Was he saying that out of pity for breaking up with me?

Do I still be friends with him or do I cut him out of my life?

Unfortunately, this is a very common scenario, not just for trans or queer folk but equally for women (people often placed in the margins). We grow up being categorised into 'dating material' or 'wife material' where affection, sex and emotional intimacy are all offered freely, but the minute things get serious, you are told you were never 'the one'.

It's a familiar pattern – dismissing the 'relationship' label but then describing it as 'special' when leaving, insisting on platonic but initiating sex, controlling the narrative, keeping their options open while keeping you emotionally attached so that they can exit when it suits them, without ever being fully accountable.

So what this guy did is not unusual, but that does not make it any less damaging.

So let's start by unpacking this one bit at a time.

Relationships like these are engineered to make you carry the guilt. You're made to feel wanted, desired, *chosen*, and when you respond with emotional attachment, that very response is used to prove that you were never suitable and you end up blaming yourself for their decisions – 'Did I do something wrong?' and 'Was I the problem?'

The first step is to stop internalising blame for someone else's emotional inconsistency. You didn't do anything wrong. Reciprocating love and wanting a relationship that promises direction doesn't make you the problem, it's a carefully designed script to keep them comfortable and keep you confused. This kind of gaslighting often hits even harder if you are a transperson.

In a society that has constantly made you believe that you're not 'enough', that has conditioned people to fetishise trans bodies, that has denied transpeople the respect of full emotional relationships, you may already carry the fear that you are 'asking for too much' by seeking both love and recognition. So when someone tells you they miss you, love your body, call you an 'amazing girlfriend' and still withdraws with excuses about marriage and children, it is easy to think the problem is you.

It is not you, it is how that identity is perceived and misused by others. You do not need to change to deserve better treatment.

You are wondering if he was just using you for sex – we can never really know what someone else is thinking, but we can see how they behave. Saying how much they care, initiating intimacy, saying you are the best girlfriend they ever had while continuing to sleep with an ex, and finally leaving because you 'cannot give him children' – that is not confusion, that is calculated breadcrumbing where someone gives you just enough affection to keep you tied but not enough to let you move forward. You were not imagining the relationship, it was real – it's just that he never planned to stay.

The more you tell yourself it was love, the harder it is to see how badly you were being played. Mixed signals are not a sign of deep feelings, they are a sign that someone does not want to commit. You need to accept that this was not confusion, it was a conscious choice he made.

Saying 'you were amazing' during a breakup is much like 'it's not you, it's me' – more of a generic term used to soften the blow so let's not focus on that. But initiating sex each time you meet and then pulling back with 'I want a platonic friendship' feels like someone just wanting to keep the door open, keep you emotionally available without the burden of offering anything real in return.

Staying connected to someone who has blurred so many lines will only extend your pain and prevent healing.

The real question is not whether he loved you – it is whether the relationship made you feel safe or left you doubting yourself more than feeling valued. Are you OK with keeping things casual or platonic? Do you feel you're being wanted or being used? And that is the point from where you need to make your decisions.

And what's most important, stop feeling guilty for wanting a loving, committed relationship.

I used to be extremely happily married to the love of my life, and we have 4 children together. She unfortunately passed away 4 years ago, and I now raise the kids by myself (successfully without boasting) and they absolutely come first in every regard.

I can't, however, allow myself to be with another woman, possibly because I don't want the kids to go through the potential loss again and possibly because no one measures up to my romanticised version of my late wife. At my age of 50 now, every woman comes with her baggage, just like I come with my own baggage, and I'm just not that attracted to 50-year-old women either.

I still have my sexual urges, and I still don't know exactly how but I now find myself hooking up with gay men for meaningless oral sex and just feel terrible afterwards. I don't want a relationship with men either, but sometimes I get confused and lonely and miss the intimacy I had with my late wife. I don't know if there is even an answer to this, or if this is just the way it will be for me now. Without fail, the gay men I hook up with tell me how many straight/married men they have sex with, and it seems to be a common taboo that no one talks about. I really don't think that the gay lifestyle or true man-to-man love is my vibe. Younger women are beautiful but make me feel like I'm the dirty old man trying to seduce the younger generation with unwanted attention. Very confused and deflated about this chapter of my life.

Grief is complex. There is no time frame and it rarely looks the way we think it should. Grief is not always about missing someone, it often shows up as guilt. And even more than that, it can become the baseline of your identity, it starts to dictate who you are, how you see yourself and what you believe you are allowed to want.

You lost the person with whom you had built your 'ideal' life, someone to share your emotional, practical and sexual self with. And with that, you lost the infrastructure within which you could be yourself without overthinking. Long-term relationships bring the comfort of routine – someone who knows your moods and cues, who shares the responsibility of family, who does not need constant explanation. That kind of comfort is not easily replicated. And because sex was part of that long-term set-up, the absence of it is not just physical, it highlights the loss of familiarity and trust that had taken years to build.

Add to that, your children have become your focus, understandably so. But in giving them a stable home, you have built up an identity of 'protector' that does not have room for vulnerability or sexual need.

But desire does not work like that. It does not disappear just because the ideal circumstances no longer exist.

Often after a loss we go through what is called the 'pedestal syndrome' – we start to preserve the memory of the person we lost in a very specific form. Your late wife cannot disappoint you any more – no more fights, no bad patches, no upheavals. Your marriage is now frozen in its best version, and that makes any potential new relationship a poor replacement (we look for faults) or even a betrayal, where you end up holding yourself back, not so much out of grief but out of misplaced loyalty because we believe that even wanting someone else would mean letting go of what you had.

But grief and desire can, and often do, coexist.

It is important to understand that sexual desire evolves with time, something that many people don't understand, and so there is a tendency to stick to what you knew, even though it's not what you want now. Desire is not 'fixed', it changes as context changes.

Perhaps you were once attracted to younger women and feel you still should be? Or perhaps younger women now represent a phase of life you miss – spontaneity and the absence of responsibility – while maybe older women seem emotionally heavier because they too have lived through difficult life events. There's no 'wrong' here, it's just your current desires reflecting your current needs.

So instead of shaming yourself, remind yourself that you are not acting recklessly, you are trying to manage real needs in the safest way you currently know. It's not about orientation but about finding something that works while being emotionally detached without running the risk of triggering guilt about 'replacing' your wife. And being told that many straight or married men do the same thing possibly makes it feel less isolating.

What next?

The first thing is to separate your grief from your sexuality. The memory of your wife will always matter, but you can still love her and have needs and also satisfy those needs.

Second, start noticing what you feel before and after these encounters. Did you need physical release here or some kind of emotional validation? Do you enjoy the sensations enough to feel that this is your moment where you can, just for a short while, shed all other responsibility? Or does it leave you feeling that you are stuck in a pattern that is not quite yours, but you do not know what else to do? If you can name what you are really looking for, you can begin to take back some control over how you make it happen.

Finally, speak to someone who specifically deals with grief, adult sexuality and single parenting to help you make sense of your feelings and needs.

PART 4
Pain During Sex

Pain during sex is far more common than most people realise, yet the stigma and shame surrounding sexuality often prevent people from seeking help. Many struggle to speak openly, even with friends, family or medical professionals, so problems that could be addressed early instead become ongoing sources of distress. At some point in their sexual lives, most people experience discomfort, but when pain becomes frequent or persistent, it is a signal that something deeper needs attention.

In this section we have tried to tackle the physical, mental and emotional causes of pain, things that are often overlooked due to lack of education.

For instance, at the most basic level, vaginal discharges are usually dismissed as trivial, but certain infections can cause inflammation and burning, leading to painful intercourse. Sexually transmitted infections (STIs) are another common cause, yet few women are encouraged to get regular checkups or are informed about how untreated infections can affect sexual comfort.

Even when no infection is present, pain can stem from lack of lubrication. Unfortunately, the line 'she doesn't need lube, I am enough for her' is more common than we would like because even today there are men who equate lube with their masculinity, meaning if she loves him, her body should provide 'enough'. As a result, women sometimes must fight to use lube simply to protect themselves from discomfort. Urinary tract infections (UTIs) can also create soreness and burning during or after sex, and conditions like vulvodynia, which is a chronic pain of the vulva without a clear medical cause, are underdiagnosed but very real.

But just as significant are the emotional and psychological roots of sexual pain. Vaginismus is one such condition where the vaginal muscles involuntarily contract, making penetration difficult or impossible. It is far more common than people realise and is often linked to emotional tension. Survivors of sexual trauma may experience vaginismus as part of their body's protective response, but it can also stem from years of being told that pleasure is shameful, that genitals are 'dirty' or that sexual activity makes one impure. These repeated messages shape the nervous system's response, creating pain even when no physical condition is present.

Anxiety and relational strain can be equally powerful triggers. If someone feels unhappy in a relationship, has unresolved conflict or feels pressured into sex, the body will articulate the refusal that they may not have been able to put into words. Arousal fails to build, the vagina remains dry or shuts down and attempts at penetration lead to pain. Even the context of sex – the stress of the first time, fear of rejection or lack of trust with a partner – can magnify discomfort. For survivors of trauma, sexual activity may bring flashbacks, dissociation or emotional distress, further reinforcing the cycle of pain.

Unfortunately, women's sexual pain is often dismissed, or worse still, it is romanticised. Pain during first intercourse is seen as proof of virginity and purity, and women are taught to expect it as inevitable. Tightness that causes discomfort is sometimes framed as 'desirable' because it supposedly benefits the partner. And when women continue to experience pain, it is brushed off as 'just how things are'.

This is deeply harmful. Pain is not a measure of virtue, desirability or sexual success. It is a clinical sign that something is wrong. The medical term for painful intercourse is dyspareunia, and it is recognised worldwide as a sexual health condition. It is treatable, but normalising pain only delays diagnosis and prevents people from seeking the help they need.

Sex is one of the few areas of health where people are still told to tolerate discomfort in silence. But pain during sex should never be considered normal. Whether it is physical (infections, lack of lubrication, UTIs, vulvodynia), psychological (vaginismus, trauma, anxiety, fear) or relational (conflict, pressure, shame), there are real causes, and there are real solutions.

Pain during sex is common but never normal. It is not a sign of purity, desirability or inevitability, it is a sign that something needs attention. The first step is acknowledging the pain rather than romanticising it or dismissing it. Seeking medical checkups for infections or conditions is essential. If no medical cause is found, psychosexual therapy can help address vaginismus, trauma or anxiety. Using lubrication, communicating openly with partners and challenging harmful myths are all practical steps that can transform sexual pain into sexual ease.

Dr Anvita Madan-Bahel

Why do some positions cause pain? I am a 31-year-old woman and I feel pain in my lower abdomen/bladder region during missionary.

Dr Allie, Sexual Health Consultant:
For far too long, women's discomfort during sex or activities related to intercourse has been dismissed as normal, with women being expected to put up with it in silence, because historically pleasure was never considered their right and speaking about pain was seen as shameful or vulgar.

Dyspareunia is the modern medical term for pain or discomfort that women might experience during, after, or because of vaginal penetration. The pain can be due to several reasons.

Sex is not straightforward. Vaginas have a slight curvature that needs to be negotiated during sex and that alone can cause discomfort during penetration. Surrounding the vagina are muscles and internal organs which can come under pressure from the angle and pace of thrusting, and conditions like fibroids, endometriosis, ovarian cysts, etc. can all heighten pain during sex.

The *Kama Sutra*, written centuries ago, acknowledges this complexity, categorising sexual positions based on the length and girth of the penis, depth of the vagina, and the physical compatibility between partners because, as it says, not all bodies fit together the same way, and pleasure requires awareness, not acrobatics.

This chapter breaks down specifically why sex can hurt in some positions, what that pain might be telling you, and how to address it.

Missionary (Face to face)

What causes pain?

Missionary is many people's go-to position, it is great as a 'gentle', 'starter' position, and can also be great for ongoing emotional intimacy, but it can cause pain from abdominal pressure or from hitting against the cervix. When a partner lies directly on top, their weight presses down on the bladder and lower abdomen, causing a dull ache or an urge to pee. Or if your legs are raised very straight, the angle allows for deep penetration, increasing the chance of the penis bumping the cervix. A tilted uterus or fibroids can also trigger sharp, crampy pain.

Solutions:

- Ask your partner to support themselves on their elbows rather than lying flat.
- Keep your legs down or plant your feet on the bed to control the angle.
- Place a small pillow under your hips to shift the pelvic tilt.
- If depth is a problem, try placing your fists on either side of your vulva to physically limit how deep or fast he can go.
- Moving your legs up and down occasionally during sex can help with micro adjustments that can shift the pain.

Doggy style (From behind)

What causes pain?

Doggy enables the penis to align directly with the vaginal canal, which allows for maximum depth. So while being extremely pleasurable it also comes with the highest risk of pain from hitting the cervix directly or pressure on the bowel. For people with irritable bowel syndrome (IBS) or rectal sensitivity this position can be overly intense.

Solutions:

- Lower your chest towards the bed to angle the cervix out of the way.
- Try prone doggy (lying flat with a pillow under the hips) to make the entry shallower.

- Make the thrusting slower and use plenty of lubrication.
- If pain persists, see a doctor for underlying issues and avoid this position altogether until the cause is treated.

Cowgirl (Woman on top)

What causes pain?

This position is often specifically recommended for pain issues because it allows you to stay in control but it requires very careful manoeuvring as it is really easy to get the angle wrong – bouncing too hard (often copied from porn) or leaning back too far can cause severe cervical impact, strain the pelvic floor, or trigger discomfort, especially if there are underlying conditions like ovarian cysts or uterine tenderness.

Solutions:
- Lean slightly forward to protect the cervix and shorten penetration depth.
- Use small, circular movements rather than bouncing up and down.
- If you feel pain, shift position or pause.

Bonus: This is one of the few positions that helps you control how to navigate the vaginal curve at your own pace, which can reduce pain significantly.

Spooning (Side by side)

What causes pain?

This is usually the most gentle position, as there is minimal weight on the abdomen and penetration is shallow. But depending on how your legs are positioned, the penis can rub against the side walls of the vaginal canal, which may be tender or inflamed. In some cases, the angle may not match the internal shape of your body and cause a scraping or pinching sensation.

Solutions:
- Try adjusting the position of your top leg – move it forward or back slightly, or place a pillow between your knees. These small shifts can make a big difference to how the penis aligns with the vaginal canal.
- This position is ideal for communicating, so use that to your advantage. Talk about how you feel to make it better.
- Use more lube.

If pain persists, see a doctor. There are multiple conditions that can cause pain relating to issues with the bladder, bowel, or genital tract that require medical attention.

Either way, do not ignore it.

Urinary tract infections

Dr Allie, Sexual Health Consultant:
UTIs are extremely common, especially in women, and one of the most frequently overlooked causes of recurring pain during sex.

It's important to understand that UTIs are not sexually transmitted infections (STIs), meaning you cannot 'catch' it from a partner, but sex can trigger it if bacteria get pushed into the urethral opening during penetration. The urethra sits just above the vaginal opening, which makes it highly vulnerable to irritation from thrusting or friction.

So this pain is not directly from the sexual organs. It comes from the urinary system, but the symptoms flare up from sexual activity, resulting in pain during sex

Most UTIs are caused by bacteria (mostly *E. coli*) migrating from the anus or vaginal area into the urethra. This can happen due to something as simple as irritation from lack of lubrication, poor hygiene, not peeing after sex, or unclean sex toys or fingers. It could happen from specific angles and pace of thrusting during sex. In some cases, a new partner's genital pH can differ enough from yours to disrupt your bacterial balance and increase the risk of infection.

Often you will experience a burning sensation when peeing or needing to pee more often, or both. However, some women do not realise they have a UTI until sex becomes really painful, and even then the cause is often misdiagnosed as dryness, lack of arousal, or bad technique. So it is important to look out for symptoms that could include burning while peeing, needing to pee frequently, a dull achy type pain in the pelvic or lower abdomen, sharp jabs during sex or soreness afterwards, bladder spasms or cramping, a bit like period cramps. If the infection spreads to the kidneys, you might also experience fever, nausea, or loin-to-groin pain.

In Ayurveda, mutrakrichha (painful urine) is identified as a serious health issue linked to an imbalance of the dosha pitta, which is associated with heat and metabolism, and could be treated with flushing the bladder and adjusting your foods to maintain internal heat balance. While we now have antibiotics to treat UTI, the World Health Organization has flagged UTI-related antibiotic resistance as a growing concern. So lifestyle-based precautions, although not the treatment, remain our best course of action – things like staying well hydrated, avoiding overly tight underwear, not holding your pee for too long can help towards better bladder health.

Many women find that they are more susceptible to UTIs even when they are in a monogamous relationship and they are both clear of infections.

Bodies are complex and there could be a number of reasons why this is happening.

Everyone carries their own set of skin and genital bacteria, which can easily mean that one person's natural flora may be more likely to trigger irritation or infection in you.

Of course inadequate lubrication remains a consistent contributor but also how we have sex with each person is different and everything can have an impact. For instance, different styles of thrusting – angle, pace, depth, etc. or positions where the legs are pinned back, like in the modified missionary – could result in more friction or pressure on the bladder and urethra, which in turn can increase risk of UTIs.

If it is the pH sensitivity to semen that is causing this, again, rinse yourself with lukewarm water after sex, to remove excess seminal fluid, and use condoms occasionally to give the body a break from exposure to semen, especially during recovery after a UTI.

And if it is the position that is causing the problem, or the angle or pace of thrusting, a really simple technique is to avoid prolonged pressure on the lower abdomen – pee before sex and learn how to place your legs or use pillows to reduce the force and tilt of the thrust (described in Chapter 31).

And finally if you are postmenopausal, speak to your doctor about vaginal estrogen. Medical science now recognises that reduced estrogen levels after menopause cause vaginal tissues to become thinner, drier, and more prone to infections, making it the leading cause of recurring UTIs in women over a certain age. Vaginal estrogen is not the same as regular hormone replacement therapy (HRT). It is a localised hormone treatment applied directly to the vaginal area, and it can significantly improve both vaginal and bladder health without affecting the rest of the body.

Just remember, whatever the cause, pain during sex should never be ignored.

Discharges and pain during sex

Dr Allie, Sexual Health Consultant:
Vaginal discharge is a normal fluid produced by glands in the vagina and cervix. It serves an important purpose in keeping the vagina clean, moist and protected from infection by maintaining a healthy pH balance.

Typically, discharge ranges from clear to whitish in colour and with no strong smell, varying somewhat with hormonal shifts, like becoming viscous or stretchy during ovulation or increasing visibly with pregnancy, arousal or birth control.

So 'abnormal' is any kind of change that is unusual compared to your typical discharge. A discharge that turns yellow, green, or grey, develops a foul odour, or becomes unusually lumpy or larger in volume is a sign that things could be wrong. And if it is accompanied by vaginal itching, burning, pain, spotting or redness, that is a definite red flag, and you should see a doctor rather than self-diagnosing.

Here are five of the most common discharge types, along with how to recognise and treat them.

Yeast infection (Candidiasis)
A thick, white, odourless discharge that looks a little bit like cottage cheese accompanied by swelling, redness or itchiness around the vulva is generally a sign of yeast infections or candida.

Candida is a fungal infection in the vagina that can occur after taking antibiotics, during pregnancy or with uncontrolled diabetes, and it can make sex quite painful. There can be a sharp pain with penetration, burning while peeing or soreness afterward. The pain is typically felt at the vaginal opening.

Candida is easily treated with over-the-counter remedies. It is generally not necessary to treat the male partner for yeast, as it's not considered an STI.

Bacterial vaginosis

A thin, milky, whitish/greyish or slightly greenish discharge with a fishy odour which can be particularly noticeable after sex or during menstruation generally indicates bacterial vaginosis (BV).

BV is caused by an imbalance in the vaginal pH and can occur in women who are sexually active but also in those who are not.

BV does not come with obvious inflammation nor does it cause pain on its own. Here the discomfort during sex is from the reduced natural lubrication that can happen due to elevated vaginal pH.

BV is treated with antibiotics. As reoccurrence is common, a maintenance therapy for a few months is sometimes prescribed. Untreated BV can increase the risk of getting other STIs and can cause complications in pregnancy. It is generally not necessary to treat male partners for BV.

Chlamydia

Chlamydia is a common STI, which can be transmitted through vaginal, oral, or anal sex and can infect the cervix and urethra as well as the sexual organs.

Most people with chlamydia are asymptomatic. But when symptoms do appear, you notice a slightly odorous, yellowish, mucus-like discharge accompanied by pelvic pain or bleeding after sex if the infection has ascended and caused pelvic inflammatory disease (PID). Pain is usually felt deeper inside due to cervical inflammation or early PID.

Chlamydia is treated with antibiotics, and it is essential that all sexual partners are treated to avoid reinfection. One should abstain from sex until the treatment is completed.

Because chlamydia often has no symptoms, be sure to get retested after about three months to ensure you haven't got it again.

Gonorrhoea

Gonorrhoea is an STI that often occurs together with chlamydia. It can infect the cervix and urethra and can also affect the rectum or throat. It's transmitted through sexual contact, and as with chlamydia, many women may not realise they have it until tested.

About 80 per cent women have no symptoms for gonorrhoea but a thick, pus-like, yellow or greenish discharge accompanied by pelvic pain and burning pee can be indicative of this. However, the symptoms can be extremely mild and easily mistaken for a bladder infection or yeast infection. So if you notice an unusual discharge or bleeding, get it tested.

Women with gonorrhoea might experience pain with deep penetration and possibly post-sex cramping or spotting. Even if there isn't strong pain initially, continuing to have sex with untreated gonorrhoea can exacerbate the condition.

Gonorrhoea needs to be treated with antibiotic injections, and treatment for all partners is essential. Gonorrhoea has become resistant to many antibiotics, so it's important to take the full course of all medications as directed by your doctor.

Can you please help me understand STIs and how they are contracted. I haven't had sex in three months but was recently diagnosed with HPV.

Dr Allie, Sexual Health Consultant:
The two most common myths around STIs are that they only happen to people who sleep around a lot and that you 'just know' when you have one. The truth is, anyone who has ever had unprotected sex, even once, can carry an STI without knowing it. As many STIs can have absolutely no symptoms, you may never know about them till it is too late.

The stigma around STIs has created a dangerous gap in education. Most people are not aware of how STIs can spread, what they feel like, or even when to get tested. And since some infections remain symptomless for years, the first sign might only appear when serious complications have already set in, like chronic pelvic pain, infertility, or in the case of HIV, life-threatening immune damage.

STIs are caused by bacteria, viruses, or parasites that are passed primarily through sexual contact, whether vaginal, oral, or anal. Chlamydia, gonorrhoea, syphilis, trichomoniasis, herpes, HPV, HIV and hepatitis B are among the most common STIs.

However, not all these require penetration to spread. Herpes, HPV and syphilis can pass through skin-to-skin contact; HIV and hepatitis B are also spread through blood; while chlamydia and gonorrhoea can transmit through oral sex as well.

Some are curable, others are manageable, but many or all of them can have serious consequences if ignored.

One of the most dangerous assumptions about STIs is that you will 'notice' them. In reality, many STIs have no visible symptoms at all, particularly in the early stages. Chlamydia and gonorrhoea, for example, are often entirely symptomless, especially in women, where the infection can remain undetected until it causes permanent damage to the reproductive system. Herpes may present as painful ulcers or a nondescript break in the skin during outbreaks, but the virus can be transmitted even when the skin appears completely normal. HPV is often silent until it causes warts or, in high-risk strains, triggers cellular changes that can lead to cervical, anal, oral or penile cancer. Syphilis classically begins with a painless sore that disappears on its own, but it can present with any symptom, such as rash, headache or abnormal liver tests, earning the title 'the great pretender' as it can be mistaken for many other medical conditions; it also gives the false impression that the problem has resolved until it returns years later, far more dangerously. HIV can remain dormant in the body for a decade, weakening the immune system slowly and silently.

STIs can cause inflammation or irritation, which can make sex extremely uncomfortable. In women it can present as abnormal discharges, cramping or pain or bleeding during or after sex. In men symptoms can include painful urination, penile discharge, or pain or swelling in the testicles. They can also present with symptoms in or around your bottom such as pain, discharge or itchiness. Herpes outbreaks can make touch painful and trichomoniasis often causes itching and burning that intensifies with friction.

Note: If sex has suddenly and inexplicably become painful for you, it is worth considering whether it could be an undiagnosed STI.

Many STIs are curable. Chlamydia, gonorrhoea, syphilis and trichomoniasis are bacterial or parasitic and can be fully treated with medication (see Chapter 33 for more information).

Other infections, such as herpes, HPV and HIV, cannot be cured but can be managed. Most strains of HPV clear on their own, but high-risk strains may require regular monitoring.

HIV can be managed with lifelong antiretroviral therapy, and hepatitis B can be controlled with medication.

STIs vary in how infectious they are. Herpes and HPV are highly contagious, even without symptoms. Chlamydia and gonorrhoea are also easily spread through unprotected sex. Syphilis is most contagious in its early stages, and HIV, while less transmissible per sexual encounter, has the most serious long-term consequences. Many of these infections can be transmitted even when the carrier has no idea they are infected.

What next?

Regular testing to know your status and protect yourself from STIs is essential, as early detection can prevent long-term complications.

If you test positive for an STI, make sure your partner is treated at the same time. Many people make the mistake of getting treated individually, only to pass the infection back and forth. Abstain from sexual activity until both of you have completed treatment and are symptom-free. Reinfection is common, but it is entirely preventable with shared responsibility.

Finally, while condoms are essential, they do not protect you against everything. Some infections, like herpes and HPV, can be spread through areas not covered by a condom. The best protection is a combination of barrier methods, regular testing and open communication with your partner. Prevention is the best way forward.

Pelvic inflammatory disease

Dr Allie, Sexual Health Consultant:
Another possible cause of pain during sex is pelvic inflammatory disease. PID is an infection of the upper reproductive tract that primarily affects the uterus, fallopian tubes and ovaries. It is most commonly caused by untreated STIs like chlamydia or gonorrhoea, but it can also happen from things like abortion, IUD insertion or anything where bacteria can travel from the vagina further into the reproductive tract.

Unfortunately, because women's pain during sex is so normalised and ignored, PID often goes undiagnosed till it shows up as a severe complication like ectopic pregnancy or infertility.

That said, the early signs of PID are so subtle – often it is just a dull, persistent ache in the lower abdomen or pelvic area – that it is easy to confuse it with period pain or even just fatigue. Neither is there a predictable pattern – it can build slowly or it could suddenly appear; it could remain as a persistent low-level ache that never quite goes away; for some it is a flare-up around ovulation, menstruation or during sex. If the infection has spread to the fallopian tubes or ovaries – especially with deep thrusting during sex – it can feel like internal cramping. Once the infection becomes established, it can cause significant damage to the fallopian tubes and ovaries and pain can worsen if it is not treated and lead to other complications.

If caught early, PID can be treated with a course of antibiotics. But since there is no isolated symptom that immediately indicates PID, there isn't a separate test for it, and doctors have to rely on clinical judgement based on symptoms and tests like internal examinations, swabs and ultrasounds.

Also, PID can develop without obvious symptoms. Silent infections, especially those caused by chlamydia, can cause the same damage over time, which is why regular STI testing is critical for anyone who is sexually active. Reinfection is also common if the sexual partner is not treated at the same time, so both partners must be included in the treatment process.

What next?
- *Journal to track your symptoms.* Because PID symptoms can be vague and the pain can fluctuate, keeping a simple log of what kind of pain, discharge or bleeding you are getting during sex can help both you and your doctor diagnose better. Note the timing, severity and context (for example, during sex, after your period, etc.) so that the information is not dismissed as 'normal cramping' or hormonal fluctuation.
- *Do not self-diagnose.* If the pain feels deep or there is unusual discharge, don't start using home remedies or self-medicating. See a doctor. Misdiagnosis delays proper treatment and increases further risks.
- *Treatment after the treatment.* Even if antibiotics clear the infection, people can come away with sexual anxiety, where sex becomes associated with pain or fear, which can lead to a different set of problems. Building strong communication with your partner is great for any aspect of your relationship but also consider counselling to help you reconnect with your body and restore confidence.

I cannot manage penetration of any kind, not even a little bit, I just freeze. I think it is vaginismus. There are some clinics that offer psychiatric help for it but it's very expensive and there are very few such places. Please can you help?

Dr Anvita Madan-Bahel:
Vaginismus may be psychological, but its manifestation is very real and very physical, and it is not solved through willpower. It is a response pattern where the muscles brace themselves against a perceived threat – past trauma, cultural shame, fear of pain, subconscious anxieties picked up over time – which needs to be understood, unlearned and reprogrammed.

This chapter offers exercises and practical tips for specific layers of vaginismus – physical, psychological and emotional – so that healing can be structured, trackable and self-led.

Mirror and breath practice
For many people vaginismus is a result of shame. The sexual organs can feel unfamiliar, almost frightening, because we have been taught to think of them as 'dirty' and most women grow up never having looked at it or even touching it. The disconnection feeds anxiety and fear. This exercise helps to reduce shame and reconnect with the body.

Technique
In a private, comfortable space use a hand mirror to observe your vulva and identify each part – clitoris, labia, urethra, vaginal opening. Rest one hand on your chest, one on your pubic bone, and breathe deeply so that you can consciously feel both areas as part of your body.

Spend five minutes daily. This helps reduce avoidance and restores a sense of ownership over your own anatomy.

Tension mapping

Many people with vaginismus will involuntarily clench their pelvic floor muscles during or often at the very thought of sex, without even realising that they are doing this. Tension mapping builds awareness of how and when the body tightens and what it feels like.

Technique

Lie on your back, knees bent, eyes closed. Now scan your body slowly and very consciously. When you reach your groin, note whether the vaginal area, buttocks or inner thighs tighten and what this does to your breath and your shoulders – are you holding your breath? Are your shoulders clenching up towards your neck?

Now try a reverse Kegel. Breathe in and gently tighten, breathe out and release the muscles as far as they will go. Repeat 10 times daily. Over time, this helps you recognise unconscious clenching in daily life and during moments of sexual anticipation.

Finger introduction

When even the thought of penetration can trigger panic or pain, this exercise will help you normalise internal touch at your own pace.

Technique

Wash hands, trim nails, lie on your back. Apply a small amount of lubricant around the vaginal opening. With the soft pad of your index finger, gently explore the outer edge. Once comfortable, try inserting just the tip, no deeper than the first knuckle. Hold for a few breaths and then slowly remove. Stop if there is sharp pain or panic. This is about building safety, not endurance.

Vaginal dilator progression

Dilators can gradually desensitise the muscles and help in consistent, controlled expansion of the vaginal canal.

Technique

Begin with the smallest dilator and plenty of lubricant. In a relaxed setting, insert the dilator slowly, only to the point where it feels manageable. Hold for 5–10 minutes while doing deep belly breathing. Practise a few times a week. Once that size feels easy, move to the next. Do not rush. This is not about being 'ready' for sex, it is about developing familiarity and comfort.

Partnered touch without expectation

One of the most damaging issues around vaginismus is that it can cause isolation and shame in relationships. This exercise restores touch and intimacy without the goal of sex.

Technique

With your partner, set aside time for non-sexual touch, fully clothed or partially undressed. Take turns touching hands, arms, hair or back, avoid genitals for now. Say out loud what feels nice or overwhelming. Do this weekly. It helps rebuild physical closeness and reduces fear that every touch will escalate into pressure.

Core and pelvic coordination

Some people with vaginismus have strong pelvic muscles, but no control over when they activate. This exercise teaches you how to shift from automatic clenching to voluntary release.

Technique

Start with diaphragmatic breathing – inhale so your belly rises, exhale slowly. Then gently tighten your pelvic floor muscles (as if stopping a flow of urine), hold for 3 seconds, and release fully. Repeat 5 times. Practise daily. This helps create a body memory of what relaxation feels like, so it can be accessed during stress or intimacy.

Safety script practice

People with vaginismus can freeze or go into panic during sexual activity and because we don't know how to interrupt that panic it can escalate very quickly and create a shutdown. It will help to have a safety script to use when needed.

Technique

Write and rehearse clear phrases like 'I need to pause' or 'this is too much for me right now'. Say them aloud in the mirror until they feel natural. Then practise with your partner in non-sexual situations. This builds your confidence to protect your limits without shame or withdrawal.

Vaginismus recovery is not linear. You could make progress but then hit a plateau or you feel fine one day and clench the next – it is part of the body relearning safety. What matters is consistency and self-compassion. These exercises are not about rushing to have penetrative sex, they are about giving you back control over your own body.

Vulvodynia

Dr Allie, Sexual Health Consultant:
Vulvodynia is a chronic pain condition that affects the vulva. The pain is felt on the outer genital parts. It is yet another condition that causes women pain during sex and is underdiagnosed and misunderstood by the medical community, partly because there is no single symptom or test for it but also because the pain is 'invisible', that is, there is no redness, discharge or swelling to 'prove' something is wrong.

It is often described as burning, stinging or sharp pain around the vulval opening; it can be constant or triggered by touch and it can occur with or without any visible irritation.

There are two broad types – unprovoked vulvodynia, where the pain is widespread and may occur at any time; and provoked vulvodynia, where pain is triggered specifically by contact, and this can happen from sex, tampon use, tight clothing and sometimes even from sitting for long periods.

Often, people are told the pain is due to an infection or a psychological issue, when in fact vulvodynia is a nerve-based condition that may stem from hormonal changes, nerve damage, inflammation, muscle dysfunction or a past injury or infection that left the area hypersensitive.

For some people vulvodynia is triggered by friction of penetration, while for others even a featherlight touch can cause the pain. In all cases the pain is described as 'disproportionate to the contact', that is, something like the merest brush with a cotton swab can feel like a sharp burn or tearing from sandpaper.

Vulvodynia is not an infection in the traditional sense and has no discharge or foul odour.

The condition can affect anyone, regardless of sexual experience or age, and the exact cause is often unknown. However, common triggers include repeated yeast infections, excessive use of scented soaps or antiseptics, hormonal contraceptives that reduce natural lubrication, and tight clothing. For some, vulvodynia can show up after a traumatic sexual experience, a gynaecological procedure or even childbirth. For others, it develops gradually and seemingly without cause.

There is no single test for vulvodynia, and diagnosis can only be made by ruling out a number of other infections, skin conditions and hormonal issues. Once diagnosed a 'cotton swab test' is commonly used – this is a process of applying gentle pressure to specific areas of the vulva to map out pain points to help differentiate vulvodynia from more general pelvic pain or vaginismus.

Treatment varies depending on the underlying cause but generally psychological interventions and pelvic floor physiotherapy are the most effective. If left untreated it can cause long-term physical and emotional issues, which in turn can lead to long-term sexual avoidance and relationship strain, especially if the pain is dismissed or misunderstood.

What next?

Friction, heat and synthetic fabrics can aggravate vulvodynia symptoms, even without direct touch. Opt for loose cotton underwear and try sleeping without underwear at night to reduce moisture buildup.

Keeping a daily log of when pain happens – during sex, after sitting or with certain clothing – can help identify patterns. Note the type of pain (burning, stinging, itching), its intensity and what makes it better or worse. This information is critical for diagnosis and treatment planning.

Because it does not show up on a lab test, vulvodynia is often overlooked. Ask for the cotton swab test to help steer the conversation towards the correct diagnosis. If your doctor is unfamiliar or dismissive, seek out a gynaecologist or pelvic pain specialist with experience in vulval pain conditions.

Sex is not a punishment or something to be endured or suffered through. If sex hurts, even a little, it is not a sign that you have to toughen up, it is a call for attention. Pain of any kind during sex should never be dismissed or normalised.

Part 5
Bodily Functions

The body and sex are deeply connected, yet ironically we rarely have a relationship with our bodies. On the contrary most people have an actively negative relationship with our sexual organs, having been taught from early childhood to think of the vagina, penis and anus as 'dirty', with so much shame, stigma and silence surrounding them that even using the actual scientific terms is taboo – using these words in a social setting would draw horrified looks and social censure. So we end up instead with a collection of nicknames, each more bizarre than the other, and this early conditioning sets the stage for awkwardness and embarrassment later in life, loading those parts of the body with taboo instead of them just being aspects of human anatomy.

And this silence has consequences, resulting in a shocking lack of sex education, where instead of equipping our kids with information and knowledge that will help them to make safe, informed decisions, parents and teachers are either too embarrassed or ill-equipped to speak about it in any kind of truly meaningful manner and many go so far as to believe that talking about is tantamount to encouraging young people to 'have' sex. As a result, many learn about sex from peers, pornography or unreliable sources, absorbing myths that can range from the absurd such as large hips or big boobs means 'she's had a lot of sex' or 'asking a guy to use a condom means she is not a virgin' to positively dangerous ideas like 'a loose vagina means she is promiscuous' and 'if she doesn't get pain she is not a virgin'. These myths create anxiety and confusion and can often lead people to make unsafe decisions, engaging in treatments or behaviours that are harmful and risky, because they fear being judged if they ask for correct information.

Patriarchal systems have been at the root of many sexual myths. By linking sex and sexuality with morality, purity and religion, they turned sex into a measure of whether someone was 'clean' or 'impure'. These ideas have laid the foundation for practices such as female genital mutilation (FGM) or the demand that women remain virgins until marriage. In essence, patriarchy maintained control over women by controlling their sexuality and their bodies.

Reclaiming that control is essential. Both women and men need to develop a relationship of respect and self-ownership with their bodies, and most importantly, with their sexual organs.

Unfortunately, far too many women have never even looked at their vaginas, let alone touched them. Their relationship with their vaginas, anuses and breasts is often shaped by the belief that these parts are dirty and shameful and must be hidden. As a result, many remain disconnected from their own anatomy and are unaware of how their bodies function.

The first step is to develop personal comfort with one's own body. Simple exercises such as looking at one's genitals in the mirror, noticing their shape and variation, or exploring non-sexual touch on different parts of the body can help reduce discomfort or embarrassment. Many people are surprised to learn how much natural variation exists in vulvas, penises and breasts. Projects such as the Great Wall of Vulvas are a great resource to understand this diversity.

Only when we build this connection and relationship with our body can we understand its needs and desires. In cases where the relationship with the body has been disrupted due to FGM or sexual violence, that too can be healed from the trauma and rebuilt. Moreover, sexuality is not confined to the reproductive organs alone, the entire body contains erogenous zones that can be explored for arousal and pleasure.

Another major roadblock is *performance pressure during sex*, which can often be more intense than performance anxiety at work or in sports.

Media images of masculinity reinforce the myth that men must be all-knowing about sex, their 'manhood' measured by their ability to be constantly ready for intercourse, aroused on demand, and capable of bringing a partner to pleasure at any time. This leaves no space for the reality that men too may not always want to or be able to engage sexually.

On the other hand, women carry the burden of performance pressure in a different form. They are expected to hold the 'magic wand' to arouse their partner, using their bodies to seduce him while being told that his erection – or lack of it – is their responsibility. If she fails to meet his needs, the narrative warns, he will 'look elsewhere' for satisfaction. Yet, at the same time, she is told she should not have sexual desires of her own and must only follow his lead.

Performance pressure is at the top of the list of things that can ruin sex lives. It not only takes away the pleasure, leaving just a joyless transactional performance, but it also impacts our ability to communicate honestly, binding us so tight in the 'shoulds' and 'should nots' that it leaves no room for sharing.

Dr Anvita Madan-Bahel

My wife is very loud, especially during climax. I understand that she is enjoying herself, but it gets embarrassing, and I have to remind her that other family members can hear us. I have asked her to be quieter and she tries, but it doesn't work. Last night I tried to press her bum to remind her about the noise during climax, but she got irritated and we ended up in an argument. I asked her to try putting a cloth in her mouth. Will that help? What should I do?

Popular media's visuals of the head bouncing 'yes, yes, yes' of women's climax has shaped how female desire is perceived and performed.

But is this real? Do women actually get loud during sex? Yes, they do. The term for noisy sex is 'copulatory vocalisation' and it is very normal for women to make all sorts of sounds to indicate their arousal or pleasure. But not necessarily in the way popular media will have you believe.

In reality, the loudest part of sex for many women is not penetration but foreplay, because this is when most women tend to orgasm. So the sounds accompanying climax are often less about a physiological reflex and more about anticipation and performance.

The *Kama Sutra* describes five distinct sounds women make during foreplay as cues that signal how their arousal is building. It was essential for anyone who wanted to be a better lover to recognise and understand these cues to know whether things were going in the right direction or when to adjust pressure and pace.

But while many women can be organically 'noisy' during foreplay, research shows that women use sex sounds at different stages of sex for different purposes. A study by Gayle Brewer and Colin Hendrie[*] found that while for some moaning

---

[*] G. Brewer and C.A. Hendrie, 'Evidence to Suggest That Copulatory Vocalizations in Women Are Not a Reflexive Consequence of Orgasm', *Archives of Sexual Behavior*, 40(3), 559–564.

may be a natural instinct, more than 50 per cent of women moan to speed up their partner's orgasm or to fake their own orgasms so they can finish quicker. But equally there are a large number of women who make loud sounds to encourage their own body to build excitement before becoming quieter as they approach orgasm. So whether by instinct or through learned behaviour, noisy sex can become an intrinsic part of your pleasure systems and cannot be switched off easily, nor should it be treated as something shameful.

However, as a partner, your discomfort is also valid. I can understand the embarrassment of family members hearing you. And although she is in no way wrong for being expressive, if it is causing you anxiety, it will not lead to pleasurable intimacy either.

Actions like pressing her body during climax or suggesting a cloth in her mouth might seem like easy solutions, but in moments of physical and emotional vulnerability, she may feel that she's being punished for enjoying herself. For you it may be a gentle reminder, for her it may feel like she's being judged, and that can take its toll on your sex life.

So rather than trying to silence her, let's find a way to shift the experience, for when done right 'quiet sex' can also be very erotic. For instance, if we can play 'silent' as erotic restraint or the thrill of 'not getting caught', you'd be surprised at how a little bit of surreptitiousness can heighten intimacy in the weirdest ways.

Try playing a 'control game' – no props or force, just words and body language. Lie them down and straddle them, your hands on either side of their shoulders, close enough that they can feel your weight but not your full touch. Look down and say with authority, 'Stay quiet. If you make a sound, I punish you.' Keep your voice low and deliberate. With that one rule suddenly every breath swings between tension and arousal. It is about watching them hold back, testing how far they can go without breaking the rule.

Or set the scene as if you are sneaking around – whispering, slow movements, a hand over the mouth – not to silence, but because 'we should not get caught'. It reframes the situation as something forbidden and exciting, instead of something awkward or shameful.

If you feel more at ease with traditional alternatives, opt for times when you think everyone may be asleep or use soft music/TV to mask the noise. If she is loudest during penetration, extend the foreplay and keep penetration time shorter, maybe you can even try slowing down the pace of thrusting. This will make the climax more mellow and will also control her noise level. And if needed, introduce playful muffling – a scarf or cushion, as you suggested – as a shared erotic tool rather than a silencing one.

And finally, try quieter positions. Some positions like seated face to face or side-by-side missionary naturally slow down thrusting. And of course *69 is great for mutual engagement and less speech.

Kissing is another great technique. If she is nearing climax, kiss her. It naturally mutes the sound while increasing intimacy.

But also a quick reminder that although noisy sex can be a problem, not everyone is lucky enough to be with someone who so clearly enjoys having sex with you. From all the messages I receive I can tell you it is a rare gift. So although we are working here to muffle the noise, remind her at the same time how much you love her and her joy in making love.

My vagina and upper thighs have dark pigmentation and they are fat and I feel very self-conscious about it. How can I have sex with this body? Should I lighten it with bleaching or cosmetic surgery? Are these options safe? My friend mentioned that dark patches in these areas are common – is that true? I cannot ask my mom – she'll kill me if she knows I'm looking at myself down there.

Many people grow up without ever being told what their genitals are supposed to look like. The result is that the first time they look at themselves, they assume something is wrong.

The beauty industry and mainstream porn have created an unrealistic standard for what constitutes 'desirable' female bodies, specifically what desirable vaginas should look like, making pigmentation around the genitals one of the most common concerns. And because no one will talk about it, instead of dispelling doubts, it has become a source of distress, shame and fear, paving the way for cosmetic procedures for parts of the body that were never meant to be altered.

So let's start with the most basic biology – it is normal for adults to have some pigmentation around their genitals. It is caused by a combination of hormonal changes after puberty, friction from tight clothing, shaving or waxing, sweating, and even weight gain. It is especially common in people with medium to dark skin tones and becomes more prominent with age.

Over the past two decades, however, the myth of the 'pink', hairless, flawless vulva has been forcefully pushed into the mainstream consciousness. What began as an adult film industry standard in California in the early twenty-first century has since spread into everyday beauty discourse with treatments like genital bleaching, acid peels, laser treatments, and DIY whitening creams, all claiming to give you the 'perfect vagina' and drumming it into women that we are only attractive if every part of our body conforms to some fictional aesthetic.

There is, of course, no equivalent demand being placed on men. And that alone should be enough to question what these treatments are about.

Let's start with your concern about 'fat' upper thighs. The upper thighs and the pubic mound naturally store more fat due to the presence of estrogen, which helps cushion movement and protect reproductive organs. It has a biological function and trying to unnaturally remove it can cause medical issues.

Similarly, most bleaching and cosmetic lightening treatments contain acids, steroids, or bleaching agents that can severely damage the skin around the vulva and inner thighs, which is extremely sensitive. Besides problems like burning, inflammation, hyperpigmentation – which ironically will cause more darkening – many people also report permanent scarring, long-term sensitivity, and pain during sex. And since many of the so-called professional laser clinics often operate without proper medical supervision or safety protocols, it means that any mistake could have lifelong consequences.

Sometimes pigmentation can be linked to conditions like eczema, fungal infections, or psoriasis. So visiting a doctor, just to rule this out, is not a bad idea. But if your only concern is that the colour of your skin in that area does not match what you have seen online, the problem is not your body, but what you have been taught to believe about it.

You ask, 'How can I have sex with this body?'

Perhaps we first need to ask whose gaze are you using to judge your body? Perhaps you have internalised the idea that your body is undesirable because it doesn't match up to the edited versions of reality that we are being fed. That may explain why you're feeling hesitant about intimacy. But the solution isn't forcing your body to live up to some unreal ideal because there will always be a new trend or standard to fit into. It's about changing the narrative to work with your reality.

One of the best ways to shed this is to dedicate some time every day to looking at yourself down there. From a very young age girls are taught to be ashamed of their bodies, and particularly to think of their genitals as dirty and shameful and something to be hidden. And then when we do manage to sneak a peak, and they look nothing like we 'imagined' they would, it freaks us out.

But the more you look at anything, the more your eyes start to get used to it, and all the little things you find distressing or anxiety-inducing will start to lose their power.

And finally, stop comparing your body to pornography or filtered social media content. These images are curated, altered, and designed to sell fantasy, not reality. Your body is real.

I pass wind during sex and it completely ruins the mood. It happens with penetration; it happens when we change positions. It is so embarrassing! I have stopped having sex because of this but that has unfortunately led to fights. My husband laughs when I pass wind but this is not my idea of sexy. I asked my mother for advice and she has told me to go for surgery because she says that if this continues he will have an affair. What should I do? Is there a solution, like surgery, or medicine? I am desperate.

The sound you're describing, the release of air from the vagina during sex, is today known as a 'queef', but it is far from being a modern phenomenon. Vaginal farts have been documented and described for centuries, with lovers and writers discussing the sounds, the positions that cause them, and the reactions they elicit.

The *Kama Sutra* even advises men to keep perfumed oils by their bedside 'in case the beloved fouled the air at night with passing wind'. Whether referring to vaginal air or flatulence, the implication was that bodily sounds were neither unnatural nor shameful but rather a normal part of the intimate landscape.

The sixth-century Arabic text *The Perfumed Garden* describes a rear-entry position in which the woman stands bent forward, hands on the floor, while the man penetrates her from behind in such a way that if she stands still and he withdraws in just the right way 'there will escape from her vagina a sound resembling the lowing of a calf'. The author goes on to remark that although men found both the position and the sound pleasurable, most women, once aware that it would result in a queef, avoided it entirely, flagging an interesting pattern that perhaps women have always found anatomical noises unfeminine and embarrassing even if their partners do not have a problem with it.

Western literature of the 18th and 19th centuries is full of euphemisms. From the 'wind of Venus' to the 'feminine trumpet' of bawdy ballads to the mock romantic 'Venus's sigh' to (possibly my favourite) 'the silent one speaks' of Victorian erotica, queefing has been referred to as everything but itself, suggesting that people have always struggled to name and normalise this harmless, natural sound.

For many women, it still feels like a breakdown of the idealised, polished version of female sexuality they've been taught to maintain, something that will ruin the mood. But men often associate it with erotic pleasure, verbalising it as their ability to 'fill her up' – modern slang for having penetrated deeply.

The truth is, the body is not silent during pleasure. Air gets trapped and released, especially during vigorous penetration or position changes, particularly where the vaginal canal expands and contracts rapidly. It's just a sound, neither erotic nor embarrassing, but the fact that it feels like so much more is why it needs our attention.

What is queefing?

Queefing is the audible release of air from the vaginal canal, most commonly during or after penetrative sex. It is not gas from the digestive tract and is entirely different from flatulence, even though it may sound similar.

During arousal the vaginal canal elongates and relaxes to enable pleasurable penetration. This creates 'space' in which air can get drawn in, especially during thrusting or shifting positions. When the muscles contract again or when a penis (or finger or toy) is withdrawn, that trapped air is released, causing what sounds like a fart. It is not odorous or unhygienic and it is generally not a medical concern either, but the thing is, it is also not avoidable without compromising pleasure.

Bodily Functions

Why and when is it likely to happen?

Queefing is more likely to happen in positions where you are opening the vagina as wide as possible to enable deep penetration, so any kind of rear entry positions like doggy style or standing penetration; inverted positions where you have your legs over your partner's shoulders or the hips are lifted considerably; or fast-paced thrusting or sudden change in positions. But equally, it can also happen in slower, gentler, and seemingly 'safe' positions.

The point is the more relaxed and open your body is, the more likely you are to draw in air, but then again that openness is exactly what makes sex feel good. So it is a case of what one is ready to compromise on.

You might be more prone to queefing depending on where you are in your menstrual cycle. Women are more likely to queef when ovulating or during their period because the pelvic floor tends to be weaker during these times, says Gabi Levi, sexpert at Shagstory.com. As to when your pelvic floor muscles are at their maximum strength? That would be during the luteal phase of your cycle, or right after ovulation and before your period, explains Dr Ingber. 'We speculate that this is due to hormonal changes during this time,' he adds. If we can just accept that queefs are a natural bodily response to shifting hormonal cycles, a part of physiology, it can make a huge difference to how we view them.

Are queefs a cause for concern?

For most people, queefing is harmless, but there are rare medical conditions (vaginal-rectal fistula, for instance) that can mimic it. If your queefing has an unpleasant odour, or you notice things like itching, bleeding, discharges, or pain, anything that is more than just the sudden passing of air, you should speak to a doctor.

The psychological load

Despite being harmless, queefing is one of those things people never forget once it happens to them, especially during early sexual experiences. It's misunderstood, often confused with flatulence, and can instantly interrupt the mood with embarrassment or laughter that is hard to interpret.

People begin avoiding positions that bring them the most pleasure. They try to contract their vaginal muscles mid-act to suppress sound, which only makes penetration uncomfortable. The sound, rather than the pleasure, becomes the focus. And sadly, this is a completely gendered discomfort. Queefing doesn't make men feel like failures, but women internalise it as a disruption of sensuality – unsexy and 'wrong'. It is neither.

Can it be prevented?

Not entirely, but if you want to minimise it for comfort and not shame, you could try small things like strengthening your pelvic floor to increase tone and control, you could work on 'partial withdrawal' where you come out a little bit at a time to reduce the vacuum effects, and possibly go with positions that feel snug rather than wide.

The most powerful fix is understanding what queefing is. Bodies make all sorts of sounds and movements during pleasure – sighs, moans, pulses, etc. This is one of them.

What next?

- *Understand the mechanics.* Queefing happens when air gets trapped and released from the vaginal canal during penetration, deep thrusting. or position changes. It is normal and harmless.
- *Name it, don't ignore it.* Trying to pretend it didn't happen often makes it worse – silence turns into shame. If it distresses you, acknowledge it with humour or lightness – not because it's funny, but because it breaks the tension.

- *Talk to your partner.* If your partner laughs, let him know it doesn't feel playful to you. Help him understand that while it may not bother him, it affects your confidence and impacts your desire for intimacy. Mutual comfort and respect is all-important.
- *Make space for games.* According to the *Kama Sutra* sex should be joyous, like playing together. Some couples find it helpful to turn the awkwardness into a shared joke – keeping score of how many times it occurred during a particular session, giving it a silly nickname, or treating it like a team moment rather than a disruption. The idea is not to trivialise it, but to take away its power to embarrass you.

Why do I find the idea of sex better than actual sex?

For many women, the idea of sex – the anticipation, the fantasy, the closeness – often feels far more exciting than the act itself and a large part of this is because of the silence that surrounds female desire. Our only exposure to the subject is the visuals of pop media, which show us what women are supposed to 'do' during sex but never what we are supposed to 'feel'. As a result, many women grow up without understanding their own arousal patterns or knowing what turns them on, which is not the wild, loud, sweaty acrobatics but rather the slow, deliberate movements and exploration that allow the body to tap into its own excitement.

Which is what happens in foreplay. You are wrapped in someone's arms, your thighs are stretched or pressed together as your excitement dictates, you can feel each other's breath, you are held as you wish to be held, you move as you wish to move. But once penetrative sex begins, your body has to follow someone else's instructions – legs are opened, hips are lifted, the focus shifts from being close to being entered. And for many women, that shift from being held to being positioned breaks the circuit of arousal.

Studies have shown that women often experience the deepest pleasure when the pelvic floor is relaxed and the thighs are closed or are able to press together, but most sexual positions create the opposite posture, emphasising performance over sensation. The erotic energy that builds in fantasy or in the closeness of foreplay dissipates when the body is suddenly asked to perform rather than feel.

Many women report feeling like sex is something that 'happens' to them rather than with them. And that makes the body withdraw even as it is being touched. So when women say the idea of sex is more exciting than sex itself, it is not because they lack desire. It is often because sex, as it is presented and expected, does not match how their bodies feel pleasure. The buildup, the fantasy, the foreplay allows you to remain in touch with your arousal; the act on the other hand often takes it away.

What next?

It's about understanding how to bridge the gap between desire and sensation. Give yourself permission to be more excited by the 'idea'. If your arousal language needs imagination and fantasy to build up desire, that's fine. Just don't finish it there, extend it gradually to your physical play as well by carefully exploring what kind of touch on what part of your body gives you pleasure. Take your time to feel it rather than just 'do' it.

Start with the body. Many women report that the shift from foreplay to penetration breaks the arc of arousal, not because the desire has disappeared, but because the posture of the body changes so dramatically. During foreplay the body has the freedom to be as it wants – held skin to skin, thighs pressed together, back arched, curled around each other in whichever way you want. But during penetration that closeness shifts to 'being positioned'. Now suddenly you have legs apart, hips tilted, arms supporting – it's about instructions and 'doing it right' and ensuring you don't have pain and a million other 'to dos' – and this can lead to a feeling of emotional or sensory disconnect.

Simple adjustments like keeping the legs closer, experimenting with positions that maintain skin contact or shifting the angle of your pelvis to preserve that feeling of closeness can help maintain the pleasure arc. This is not about 'trying harder' to enjoy sex, it is about understanding how the body wants to feel pleasure and building the act around that.

If you notice that your arousal peaks when your thighs are closed or your legs stretched out, etc., adjust your position to allow that. Add some whispered conversation or mutual laughter, keep the mind engaged, which in turn will help keep the body responsive.

It's also worth exploring what it is about the fantasy that feels so much more exciting – is it the novelty, the emotional connection or the sense of freedom? Once you identify it, include it in your real-life sex – and I don't mean by role playing, just start with what kind of tone, touch or language excites you so that he can try and do it for you. Build it from there.

Having said that, I want to point out that real sex often does not match imagined sex – not because it is less, but because it is different. Real sex can be quiet, awkward, tender, slow, funny, underwhelming and hard work. If you are waiting for it to feel like fantasy – explosive, cinematic, overwhelming – it is always going to feel anticlimactic.

I also want to add that perhaps this disconnect goes a lot further back than present-day media representation. It is not just the idea of sex versus the act of sex, but 'man' versus our idea of a man.

For many women, the idea of a man's attention, his gaze, his imagined presence is far more arousing than his actual body in the room. For centuries, female arousal has been shaped by stories of courtship, longing, stolen glances, waiting to be chosen. Women were taught to desire 'being desired', we are not taught to desire the body of a man. The erotic thrill was in what might happen, not what is happening.

Also, men's bodies have not been eroticised in the same way women's have. In most visual and cultural narratives, the male form is rarely presented for female pleasure, it is a symbol of power, not sensuality. So the female brain has been socialised to respond more to his attention than his physical form.

The physical body of a man may be fabulous but may not trigger desire directly – it could instead be how he moves, speaks, looks at you, holds back or touches you that stirs excitement. As an experiment, change how you see the male body, not by forcing yourself to 'find it hot' but by discovering his texture, his scent, the warmth behind his knees, the softness of the inner wrist. Learn his body, rather than just being with it.

But also importantly if something feels consistently off – physically or emotionally – you may need medical intervention. Sometimes what feels like disinterest or disconnect may be caused by lack of arousal, hormonal shifts or emotional exhaustion and you may need to see a doctor.

I feel like you're the only person who can answer this question for me. Firstly, I'm scared of sex because I have a lot of trauma around sex but also I have unfortunately been through female genital mutilation and I don't know if you know that there are 4 types of female genital mutilation and I have been through the third type which means I don't have any clitoris and I don't know how to have any orgasms and I have never had any orgasm in my life so I don't know how it feels. I also tried masturbating but everything that goes in me feels like a threat and I don't know how to calm my body. I feel like my body is not mine any more and I feel like a freak among my friends. Do you have any solution or suggestions to how I can masturbate without any clitoris?

Masooma Ranalvi, FGM Survivor and Co-Founder, WeSpeakOut:

What you have experienced – the physical trauma of FGM, resulting in emotional fear around sex and intimacy, and the feeling of being shut out of your own body – is very real and very understandable. And while it can feel isolating, you should know that you are not alone, there are people and communities around the world who can support you in processing what has happened.

But for now, let us start with what can be done here.

As you said, there are four recognised types of female genital mutilation. Any form of genital mutilation is a direct violation of a woman's body carried out simply to satisfy patriarchal ideas of purity, control, and honour. It is inhuman in the extreme and there can be no justification for it.

But type 3, which you went through, is considered the most severe. Here, typically the labia minora is cut, the clitoral glans removed, and then the remaining tissue pulled together and stitched to cover the vaginal opening, leaving only a narrow hole just enough for urine or period blood to pass through. So this is not just about the pain of physical injury, there is also scar tissue, nerve exposure, and psychological trauma, all of which impact how the body processes sensation and how the nervous system responds to touch or intimacy.

The entire aim of this type of FGM is to seal the vulva shut, making penetration extremely painful or even impossible.

Add to this painful scar tissue and nerve exposure. Removing the clitoral glans does not deaden the area. On the contrary, the damage can make it hypersensitive to touch and pain. So it doesn't just reduce pleasure, it makes sex cripplingly painful.

And finally the distress of feeling unsafe when anything enters the body and feeling tense even when you are by yourself. Your body learned at a very young age that 'touch' meant danger – from the physical pain it caused or from being punished by an adult for touching yourself or the instilling of cultural and social norms of 'inappropriate' sexual behaviours.

So now when you try to touch yourself or imagine someone else doing so, the nervous system reacts with survival memory – it tenses, prepares for pain, and shuts down sensation to protect you.

I can also understand your grief at never having experienced an orgasm. So much of our sexual identity is built around that rush of pleasure that when it seems out of reach it can feel like something essential is missing.

However, the loss of the clitoral glans does not mean that pleasure is impossible. Every part of the body can be an erogenous zone depending on how you touch it – breasts, waist, belly button, spine, back of the knees. Also, the clitoris itself is larger than just the visible part, and even if the glans is missing (depending on the extent of the cutting and nerve damage) the internal branches of this miraculous little organ remain sensitive and are capable of generating pleasure.

You can get to the internal parts by gently pressing on the perineum (the area between the vaginal opening and the anus) from the outside or, if you feel brave, by inserting a finger just inside the vaginal entrance and curving it downward in a slow rocking motion towards the back wall.

But of course, to even begin this journey, you must first feel safe in your body. You cannot explore pleasure if your nervous system is still in defence mode. So the first step to masturbation is not masturbation, it is building safety. That means learning how to calm your body and notice what feels manageable in order to reintroduce touch in a pleasurable way.

Start with using a soft cloth or warm oil to stroke your arms, face, legs, etc. to see which part you can touch without triggering fear. Be aware of your breath as you do this. If it becomes unstable, try some simple breath-calming exercises. Gradually increase to experimenting with touch around the inner thighs, belly, and hips. If at some point you wish to explore the genital area, do so with care. You are not looking for a specific reaction, the aim is to just take note of your body's reaction – discomfort, panic, or relaxation?

If possible, work with a trauma-informed therapist.

Some survivors also explore surgical options. Deinfibulation (reopening the sealed vaginal opening) could potentially relieve pain, and clitoral reconstruction surgery is slowly becoming more widely available.

Many survivors of FGM eventually do find ways to experience pleasure, whether through emotional or physical means or a combination of both. Your body may respond differently from others', but that does not mean it won't.

I have got used to squeezing my thighs together for my orgasm since I was a child, which is a wonderful feeling, but now I can't orgasm any other way. When we have sex I can't feel the pleasure, I feel the need to close my thighs and press them together. And if I can't do that my pleasure disappears. Is something wrong with me, what should I do? How can I improve my sex life?

Most girls first discover pleasure not through touch but through movement – rocking, rubbing, or squeezing their thighs together. This often begins unconsciously in early childhood, often as young as three, long before they have begun to understand what sex or masturbation even is. Especially in cultures where privacy and sexual awareness are lacking, this becomes a discreet and easy way to access bodily pleasure because it requires very little – no toys, no getting undressed, no visible movements, and no knowledge of anatomy.

The 'squeezing thigh' pattern is extremely common. It is not a dysfunction. It is simply a habit built over time where your body learns a specific script for pleasure and clings to it because it works. But the more it is repeated, the harder it becomes to respond to anything else.

And so during sex, when your legs are open and the sensations are spread out instead of focused inward, your arousal does not feel like your arousal. You find yourself willing it forward but then lose it again because the body is waiting for a cue that never comes, that familiar squeeze, that exact pressure, and without that the orgasm remains out of reach.

The unfortunate side effect is that women often feel anxious or disengaged during sex because they know they won't experience pleasure in this manner, so sex becomes an emotionally distant 'act', with faking or even visible displeasure, which in turn ends up leaving partners feeling rejected or confused, leading to resentment on both sides.

In truth, this is possibly one of the most solvable sexual problems because, remember, we are not trying to 'unlearn' anything, this is not about abandoning a deeply ingrained habit that gives you so much pleasure, it's about expanding your range. You can still love the way your body responds to thigh pressure; we are just going to teach it how to open up to other sensations as well.

What next?
Start with masturbating differently. Experiment in an open position, and if that is completely impossible, place a pillow between your thighs to keep them open, and making sure not to squeeze. This gives your body a chance to feel pleasure without always needing to clamp down.

Combine your usual technique with new ones. Edge close to orgasm in your usual way, then pause, open your thighs slightly, and breathe through the plateau without finishing.

Communicate. Explain to your partner that you are retraining your arousal. Let them know that you may need time and that you may need their help in exploring different positions or pressures.

Be patient. Your orgasm is not faulty, it is just 'specific'. You are trying to retrain your habits, and that takes time.

If you are the partner of someone who can only orgasm by pressing her thighs together, you may well be feeling confused, left out, or even hurt by the fact that you are not a part of her 'pleasure experience'. Remind yourself that this is not a rejection of you, it is simply her body's learned response, and it dates back long before you entered her life. Your role here is not to 'fix' her but rather to support her with patience and love as she learns new pleasure pathways.

Find ways to have sex that allow her to press her thighs together, like the doggy position, to see if that helps.

Or take sex off the table temporarily with non-goal-oriented positions, like spooning, straddling, or side by side with a pillow between her legs that can give her the pressure she's used to while still being physically close to you. Ask her to show you how she touches herself to see if you can co-create pleasure rhythms.

Does the vulva come out with masturbation?

This is a common concern and, like most things to do with 'cosmetic' expectations, a complete myth.

The vulva is not a hard structure. It is made up of soft, elastic tissue that changes with age, hormones and arousal.

Often people only really begin noticing their labia after they start masturbating, and when it does not look like what they have been given to believe (in mainstream porn, for instance), they assume something has 'come out' or been damaged permanently.

What many people refer to when they say 'the vulva is coming out' is the labia minora – the inner lips – which can vary hugely from one person to the next. For some, they stay tucked within the outer lips (labia majora); in others, they are naturally protruding, sometimes well past the outer lips. This has nothing to do with masturbation, it is simply different body types. It is possible that nothing has 'changed' and that this is simply the first time you looked at yourself there with attention.

But, yes, masturbation does cause a temporary visible change. When you masturbate or become aroused, blood flows to the genital area. With this, the labia swells, the clitoris becomes engorged, and the vaginal canal relaxes and widens slightly to accommodate penetration. These changes are part of the normal sexual response cycle. After orgasm, the tissue gradually returns to its resting state. But at the point of arousal you may notice that your labia is more visible or differently shaped than before. This is not a 'side effect' of masturbation. It is the normal response of a healthy body to arousal – the vulva is *meant* to unfold, stretch, and enlarge.

But some labia minora naturally extend beyond the outer lips, regardless of arousal. There is no standard shape or size and certainly no 'correct' one. Some look like a long petal, others are small and tucked in, some are smooth while others are uneven, some can be highly pigmented while others not so much. What changes over time is not the vulva itself, but your familiarity with it.

Unfortunately, because most of us are not shown what real vulvas look like, these normal variations are often mistaken for 'damage' or 'overuse'. Pornography and cosmetic beauty standards have trained us to believe that only one kind of vulva exists – small, pink, symmetrical, and tightly tucked in – and anything else is abnormal. And the genital cosmetic surgery industry with its procedures and products has added to the anxiety around labia visibility, with women feeling that 'different' means they need to be fixed. So while education remains silent, shame and comparison get louder.

So let's begin with some essential education.

Understand the anatomical structure and names of the genitalia. The vulva includes the outer labia (majora), inner labia (minora), clitoral hood, clitoris, urethral opening, and vaginal opening. Use a mirror to see what they really look like. Look at yourself during rest time and arousal time to observe what changes and what stays the same.

Now visit online sources like the Labia Library (created in Australia), which offers a large collection of unedited, non-sexualised images of diverse vulvas, shown in a clinical and body-positive light. There are also vulva casting projects, like the artist Jamie McCartney's Great Wall of Vulva, which document the extraordinary range of real, living bodies. It is important to understand that bodies have diversity and that there is nothing wrong with you.

If you feel ashamed about 'loose' or 'hanging' labia, ask yourself where that idea came from, who decided what was normal, and who gains by your insecurity.

While 'change' is not 'damage', if something hurts or feels uncomfortable or inflamed, go see a doctor.

Just to reiterate, masturbation does not cause your labia to 'come out' or grow longer or become discoloured. But because it brings you into contact with a part of your body that most of us were taught to ignore or hide or be ashamed of, that sudden awareness of it can be frightening, especially if no one is explaining this to you.

Last night in the hostel a bunch of us started discussing the hymen – like, is it supposed to tear, does it actually tear? What happens when you have sex? We googled it and came up with so many different answers and ideas that it got even more confusing. Please can you explain this properly for us.

Dr Pritha Dasmahapatra, Gynaecologist and Obstetrician:
Since time immemorial, the hymen has been a symbol of morality, honour, and sexual history for women. Whether it is the expectation of bleeding during first-time sex or the use of virginity tests to judge 'purity', the myths surrounding the hymen have caused real psychological and physical harm. The truth, however, is far simpler and far less dramatic – the hymen is a thin, variable piece of tissue with no known medical function, with no behaviour pattern, and absolutely no connection to sexual history.

What exactly is the hymen?
The hymen is a thin, frilly tissue located at the vaginal opening. It does not 'cover' the vaginal opening like a 'seal' or a 'door', nor does it wrap like cling film, waiting for some kind of sexual encounter to 'break' it.

There is no definitive shape to the hymen. Just like every other part of the body, hymens come in different shapes and sizes.

- Ring-shaped – the most common type
- Crescent-shaped – open on one side
- Microperforate – with several small holes
- Septate – a thick band of tissue across the opening
- Imperforate – no opening at all (which is rare and would block period flow)

If a hymen is completely closed off (imperforate) or causes physical discomfort or blocks menstrual flow, a minor surgical procedure is needed. But in most cases, these variations are normal and harmless.

Hymenal tissue is generally soft and insubstantial, similar in texture to a damp tissue, meaning it can tear easily and, for many, it recedes or fades on its own with age. Some people are born with very little hymenal tissue, some with none at all, and for most, it gradually thins out and disappears due to hormonal changes during puberty and later life.

Does it 'break' during sex?
No. This is one of the most persistent myths. The hymen is not a seal that 'breaks' during penetration. In many people, it stretches over time due to daily physical activity like sports, cycling, dancing, masturbation, or even medical checkups, and so it does not exist anyway. Sometimes it may tear slightly during sex but for most people this is not even noticeable.

The expectation that there must be pain and bleeding the first time one has sex is not only incorrect but dangerous. The hymen has very few blood vessels, so even if there is a tear, bleeding is often minimal or absent. The reasons for bleeding and pain are more often dryness, lack of arousal, anxiety, infection, etc.

Is there a link between hymens and virginity?
Absolutely not. Virginity is a social concept, not a medical condition. The idea that the state of someone's hymen can prove their sexual history is false and has been repeatedly disproven by medical science. You cannot tell if someone has had sex by examining their hymen. Even a gynaecologist, during an internal examination, cannot determine this.

There is no such thing as a reliable or ethical 'virginity test'. These so-called tests are unscientific, abusive, and often a violation of human rights. They perpetuate control and shame, especially over women's bodies, by pretending anatomy can be used to determine morality.

What does the hymen actually do?
Medically speaking, it does nothing. There is a theory that it might offer some protection against infections in infancy, but this has never been proven. In adulthood, it serves no anatomical purpose. It does not impact menstruation, sexual pleasure, pregnancy, or childbirth. As we age, the hymen thins out, fades or breaks down entirely due to hormonal change – even without any sexual activity. Depending on your age, your hymen may have disappeared regardless of whether you are celibate or not.

In most people the remnants of the hymen eventually turn into small skin tags at the edges of the vaginal canal. This is completely normal and does not require any treatment.

What is hymenoplasty?
Hymenoplasty is a cosmetic surgery to 'recreate' the hymen by stitching the tissue back together. It is performed in some communities to allow partners to see the woman in pain or 'appearing to bleed' to satisfy a barbaric patriarchal narrative and meet a fabricated standard of virginity.

Let us be clear – this procedure serves no medical purpose, has no medical value, and is an entirely unnecessary operation with potential for negative health outcomes. Surgical risks can include pain, excessive bleeding, infection, and even sexual dysfunction. In some countries, hymenoplasty and virginity testing are illegal, and both the doctor and the initiator can be imprisoned. WHO considers it a form of sexual violence.

Can you see a hymen?
I have had women write to say that they are living through hell because their partners checked their hymen on the 'first night' and found it 'not satisfactory'.

In fact, as the hymen has no distinct shape and is the same colour as the surrounding tissue, there is no way anyone can ascertain its presence by peering into a vagina with one's phone torch to check for some kind of imaginary seal. Yes, it can be checked by a doctor during an internal examination, but even this cannot tell you anything about a person's sexual history.

Looking or feeling for a hymen to determine 'purity' only to wrongly accuse or shame someone is an abhorrent practice based on nothing but misinformation.

So why are we still talking about it?

Because the myth persists. Far too many young people are still asking whether they should bleed or not, parents are still worrying about it and prospective partners still believe they have the right to 'check'. Unfortunately, it continues to cause unnecessary shame, anxiety, and violence.

Knowing the facts is the first step in undoing this damage. The hymen is simply one more variation in human anatomy, one that plays no role in pleasure, fertility, or identity. It's time to ditch the myths.

Is there such a thing as a loose vagina? Does the vagina become loose with sex?

The vagina is a muscular, elastic canal designed to expand and contract. It can comfortably accommodate a tampon, a penis, or a baby and then return to its usual shape. It does not permanently stretch from penetrative sex, nor does it get 'loose' from having sex regularly or with multiple partners. That idea is not just false, it is medically absurd.

Unfortunately, the idea of a 'loose' vagina is one of the oldest and most damaging myths perpetuated about women's bodies.

Over time the vagina may feel different, perhaps be less responsive either to sensation or even in the way it can 'grip', but this is about muscle tone, not size. Vaginal muscles, like any other muscle in the body, can become lazy over time due to age, lack of use, hormonal changes, or childbirth. The drop in estrogen after menopause can make the tissues thinner and less elastic, childbirth can leave the vaginal muscles feeling sore or fatigued – none of this means that the vagina is 'damaged' or no longer capable of pleasure. The weakness is not permanent, and postpartum and age-related muscle loss can be reversed with simple exercises because the body is *designed* to recover.

For partners complaining that the looseness is obvious because it is causing a lack of sensation, it is worth understanding that not all lack of sensation is due to a 'faulty vagina'.

Men can experience reduced sensation because of their own physiological, psychological or health reasons. Performance pressure, anxiety, poor circulation, unhealthy diets, varying penis sizes, all contribute to reduced pleasure. Blaming the partner's vagina is both unfair and unjust.

Another crucial detail missing from our sex education is that orgasms are not *created* by 'tightness', or how much friction the vagina can create against a penis. They are the result of rhythmic contractions of the pelvic floor, the clenching and releasing of the muscles in the sexual organs to mimic pulsing. That means the more toned the muscles and the more they can respond to your command to pulse, the more powerful the climax.

In ancient erotic traditions, women were taught to consciously control the vaginal muscles to create higher levels of stimulation and pleasure, for themselves and their partners. The *Ananga Ranga*, a classical Indian text on love and intimacy, refers to the practice of sahajoli, a technique that taught women how to lift and release the vaginal muscles in specific rhythms, almost like a dance, to build control and enhance pleasure.

Today it is known as pompoir, or the 'art of the vaginal grip'. It involves isolating the ring-like muscles inside the vaginal canal and learning to pulse them in waves. Women who mastered this practice were considered highly skilled and desirable lovers, not because they were 'tight' but because they had enough command over their own anatomy to control how their muscles functioned.

Unfortunately, we seem to have replaced this tradition of building muscle tone and health with shame, silence, and surgeries that promise tightness but deliver nothing of meaning.

What weakens the pelvic floor? Age, lack of movement or use, pregnancy and childbirth, chronic coughing or constipation, poor posture, even overtightening (clenching out of habit or anxiety) can cause dysfunction.

The good news is this is not permanent.

The pelvic floor muscle is the muscle that lifts your organs, controls your bladder, grips during penetration and creates the spasms of orgasm. You do not need surgery – surgery does not fix muscle tone – you just need to re-energise your muscles.

These muscles respond brilliantly to targeted exercise, especially when you know how to do it correctly. My suggestion would be to work with a pelvic floor therapist to get yourself healthy again.

In the meantime, here is an exercise to start with. This exercise is not about arousal but rather about control and confidence. The vagina is not a mystery. If you want to understand this part of your anatomy your first step is to touch it and become familiar with it.

Find yourself a quiet, private, safe space. Make sure your hands are washed and nails carefully trimmed.

Lie down or prop yourself up comfortably,

Insert two fingers gently into your vagina, up to the second knuckle.

Breathe in and then as you breathe out try to lift your pelvic floor. Imagine the base of your body drawing up and in, as if you were trying to stop urinating midstream. You should feel the muscles gently hug your fingers and lift them slightly. This is the muscle group we are working with.

Hold that squeeze for 3–5 seconds, then release completely. The release is just as important as the contraction. Feel the muscles let go. Repeat 5–10 times. Start with what you can manage. You will build strength over time.

Advanced variation: Try a pulsing rhythm squeeze and release rapidly, like a flutter. Or lift in slow stages, like an elevator rising floor by floor, then slowly descending. These help with both strength and control.

You need to understand the difference between tightness and tension. A constantly clenched muscle is not a strong one, it is a fatigued one. What you want is a rhythmic pulsing movement, not permanent grip.

Remember there is no medical condition called 'loose vagina'. Vaginas stretch and recover. What you are feeling is muscle tone, not sexual history.

Pelvic floor muscles can weaken over time, but they can also become stronger and more responsive, and even more orgasmic. You can start strengthening them at any age.

If your partner is complaining about sensation, the issue might not be your body. Talk about all the options listed above, especially exploring pelvic floor exercises together.

As a guy, how can I prepare emotionally for first-time sex?

This is a genuinely important question, and I'm glad you're asking it.

Historically, male sexuality has been defined and measured by performance, erection, stamina, and technique. Popular media too portrays the 'man' as always in control, even when he is in love. He initiates, he knows what to do without asking, he performs without hesitation, and there is no space for tenderness – sex is about conquest not connection.

And between popular media and entrenched patriarchy this narrative is absorbed very early in life – young boys grow up believing that to be a man means to perform and to dominate.

Because this is so rarely discussed, many men go into their first sexual experience thinking they are the only ones ever to feel nervous, and if they cannot get hard immediately or find themselves hesitating, it means something is wrong with them.

And so, much like women have learned to fake orgasms, men learn to fake confidence during sex, pretending they are fine when their body is overwhelmed or frozen.

So if you are asking how to prepare emotionally for your first time, you are already half the way to changing a completely toxic narrative that does not serve anyone.

- Define 'preparation'. Preparation does not mean perfection. Let go of the pressure to perform or impress. You're not staging a show, you're trying something new. You are allowed to laugh, to ask questions, to take breaks, to get overwhelmed. You're allowed to be awkward. None of that makes the experience any 'less', it makes it real.
- Ditch the pressure to make it 'memorable'. No matter how experienced you become, sex will never look 'film

perfect'. Unrealistic expectations can trap you in a downward spiral. Instead, aim for 'happy sex', sex that feels pleasurable, exploratory, and emotionally safe, even if it's clumsy or over faster than you thought or if you had to stop halfway. If you finish feeling a little more connected to yourself and your partner, that's a great first time.

- The real preparation, as you have rightly asked, is not physical, it's emotional. That means getting clear on what this moment means to you. Are you doing this because you feel ready? Because you feel connected to your partner? Or because you think you're 'supposed to' at this age or stage in life?
- Once you have had that conversation with yourself, have it with your partner. Talk about expectations, comfort levels, boundaries. Do not assume you are on the same page. Some people attach huge emotional importance to first-time sex, believing it should be with the person they plan to spend the rest of their lives with, while others see it as more casual. A five-minute conversation beforehand will do more for your confidence than any technique.
- Start slow. Not just physically, but mentally. Take time to notice what feels good for both of you. Slow down when you need to. Pay attention to your breath, to the small touches, the small moments of intimacy. Foreplay is not a warm-up exercise, it is sex. Penetration, if and when it happens, is just one part.

No matter how much you build it up, no matter how excited you are or how much effort you have both put into the arousal, you may still encounter erection issues.

It's possible you may get hard too early and lose the erection before anything starts or you may not get hard at all because of the pressure you are under. Or you may climax within seconds, or not at all. All of this is normal. And not just the first time, it could happen the first few times.

I want to stress here that none of it is 'failure', it's simply how your body works, it happens to everyone. What matters is how you respond to it.

The worst thing you can do is start blaming yourself. Because that will make it harder the next time. If you can be kind to yourself in that moment, that's real emotional readiness.

If things don't go according to plan, don't panic – breathe, pause, laugh, and try again later. If your partner responds with care and sensitivity, you will know you are in safe company. If not, you will have learned something important about them.

What next?

Learn how your body reacts to pressure before the moment itself. Spend time understanding your body outside of partnered sex, what calms you, what overstimulates you, how your arousal responds to mood or fatigue. This is not about 'practising' performance, it is about recognising how your body behaves under different emotional states so you are not caught off guard.

Set the atmosphere to support, not challenge, your nervous system. Your environment plays a role in how safe or exposed you feel. Choose a space that feels private, unhurried, and free from potential interruptions. It is not about candles and music but about emotional comfort. Turn off your phone, draw the curtains, do whatever helps you feel grounded.

Agree beforehand on a way to pause or slow things down. Many people freeze or overcompensate when things start to go wrong. Have a simple phrase ready, like 'can we slow down for a moment', so that either of you can reset without anxiety. This is a useful technique borrowed from BDSM practices.

Do not try to mimic porn. Porn is scripted for viewer pleasure not doer pleasure. In real sex, watch for subtle changes in breath, the body softening or tensing, a pause in rhythm.

This is a big moment, but it's not an exam paper, you're not being graded. The best thing you can do is show up with self-awareness, patience, and the willingness to learn, not just about sex but also about how you show up in intimacy.

Contraception

Nse. Theodore, Contraception Advisory:
With a wide range of contraceptive options available, it is essential to understand how each one works, what it is best suited for and how different bodies may respond – because no two people experience contraception in exactly the same way.

The most widely used options are contraceptive pills, condoms, copper IUDs (coil), hormonal IUDs and contraceptive implants.

Oral contraceptive pills are among the most common methods. They come in two main types – the combined pill (estrogen + progesterone) and the progesterone-only pill (POP). Your lifestyle and medical history such as BMI, smoking and blood pressure help determine which is suitable. For example, those with a BMI over 35 are usually not prescribed the combined pill due to increased risk of blood clots.

The POP must be taken daily and becomes over 99 per cent effective when taken at the same time each day. Some pills have a 3-hour window, others 12 hours – if you are late beyond this, protection is lost.

If a dose is missed or delayed, take it as soon as you remember, then continue your next pill at the normal time, even if that means taking two in one day. To course correct you need to take 3 pills consecutively (in 48 hours).

Hormonal contraceptives often raise concerns about weight gain or fertility loss. Neither is universally true. Some people may notice temporary weight changes, and fertility may take time to return, but it does come back. That is why clinical assessment is crucial before starting a method. Even among pills, different hormone combinations produce different effects in different bodies.

Emergency pill or the i-pill is only effective if taken before ovulation occurs. However, since ovulation timing can be unpredictable, especially under stress, it is often still given. There are two types of emergency pills – the 72-hour pill and the 120-hour pill.

Body weight can impact effectiveness of the emergency pill. From 70 kilos on effectiveness begins to decline and from 85 kilos it reduces significantly. In clinics, a double dose may sometimes be offered to increase effectiveness.

Nausea is common, but if vomiting occurs within 3 hours, another dose is needed.

Condoms are the only form of contraception that protect against both pregnancy and STIs. They are easy to access, work immediately and are up to 98 per cent effective with correct use.

The most common cause of condom failure is incorrect use. Always use on an erect penis, pinch the tip before putting it on to leave space for ejaculation, and avoid tearing the packet with nails or sharp objects. Check the expiry date and that the packet is undamaged. Oil-based lubricants can weaken latex, especially during anal sex, so always use water- or silicone-based lubes. Do not store condoms in heat or tightly folded up and crammed into wallets for long periods.

Using two condoms at once does not double protection. On the other hand, it increases friction and raises the risk of tearing.

A condom must be worn before any genital contact, not just at penetration. Many rely on the pull-out method or delay wearing a condom until midway through sex, which is risky. During ovulation, vaginal mucus becomes thinner and more fertile, and since precum can contain sperm, pregnancy can occur even without full penetration or ejaculation.

The copper IUD is hormone-free, so it does not affect mood, weight or ovulation. The only difference between a

3- and 8-year version is the amount of copper wound on the device. An expired coil is not dangerous, but its effectiveness cannot be guaranteed, and it should be replaced on time. However, the copper IUD can cause heavier or more painful periods, especially in the first few months, which is why it is not recommended for those with a history of heavy bleeding or endometriosis.

The hormonal IUD works by releasing a low dose of progesterone that thickens cervical mucus in order to block sperm. Side effects include irregular bleeding initially, often followed by lighter or absent periods over time.

The main risks of IUDs are related to insertion. A vaginal swab is often done before fitting to rule out infection, which could otherwise worsen. The IUD can sometimes be expelled by the body either partially or fully, which may cause cramping or irregular bleeding. If it silently displaces, that is, if it happens without any symptoms, you may no longer be protected and there is risk of ectopic pregnancy if fertilisation occurs. Expulsion is more common in people with fibroids or very heavy periods.

There is also a rare risk of perforation (puncturing the uterine wall) during insertion. This is more likely in people who are breastfeeding or have recently had a C-section, which is why a waiting period may be advised. Signs of IUD displacement include missing or lengthened strings, unexpected bleeding, pelvic pain or your partner feeling the device during sex. If you experience any of these see a doctor immediately.

After IUD removal, fertility can quickly return, which is why clinics often advise using condoms for 7 days before removal, as sperm present in the uterus can still cause pregnancy if unprotected sex has occurred.

The contraceptive implant, now available in India's family planning system, is a small, flexible rod placed under the skin of the upper arm. It releases progesterone steadily and is over

99 per cent effective for up to 3 years. Unlike the i-pill, its effectiveness is not affected by body weight. However, it can cause irregular bleeding, and some women may stop getting periods altogether for the full duration of use.

I am 33 years old, married for 10 years. I've never experienced orgasm in our relationship. In the past, I was in an abusive relationship, where, surprisingly, the humiliation and certain behaviours in bed helped me reach orgasm.

Over the years I have shared my needs with my husband but he's uncomfortable with certain dynamics and I respect his boundaries. I really want to experience pleasure and intimacy with my partner in a way that doesn't involve humiliation or abusive dynamics. I would love your guidance on how to navigate this within a healthy, loving relationship and work towards a satisfying sex life that honours both our boundaries.

Just to show you that you are not alone, here are a few other messages I've received:

'I was 24 when I got married. When he was in a bad mood he would r@pe me and the more I cried the more he did. Over time I started orgasming in this even though I hated him and the violence. It's like my brain shut down but my body woke up. Now I can't do any else way.'

'My partner's fetish was to spit on me and call me names and tell me I was worthless during sex, so I started to fake it to finish it quicker. But now I actually orgasm like this. Why?'

'I was SA as a child by my father and uncle and I would hate it but always climax. My boyfriend says that it obviously means I wanted it because even now I use that in my solo pleasure. Is that true? Am I sick?'

Pleasure often begins with desire, and for desire to build you need love (a base of care and attraction), emotional safety (no fear, pressure or judgement) and a sense of being truly desired. But orgasms are the result of intensity of sensation – a combination of tension and stimulation.

Intensity is not always romantic or sweet. In fact, most people's fantasies are not about comfort or tenderness. They are about risk, power, taboo, because these emotions generate a stronger charge in the body. When you imagine something that shocks or frightens you in a certain way, you get an adrenaline spike – your heart races, your breathing quickens, your pelvic floor tightens and this builds intensity.

For survivors of abuse, this threshold is often built through fear, humiliation or powerlessness because, in an attempt to survive, the body converts that unbearable pressure into physical release, something tolerable, or even momentarily pleasurable, because that was the only option.

And this then becomes what we now call an 'arousal template'. The body doesn't differentiate between intensity from joy or fear. All it knows is that the charge is high. You've brought your body to that point, it's now easy to convert it to an orgasm – it's reliable, you know it can bring you to orgasm, so in the heat of the moment you automatically tap into that.

And these templates often contain elements that are really uncomfortable – being watched, being forced, being degraded. You don't want any of this in real life, but because they create the exact intensity, the body learns to recognise them as a precursor to orgasm, and it becomes our go-to for climax.

This is why so many people feel confused by their own fantasies – in a loving, respectful relationship but needing to imagine something rougher, darker or taboo to climax. This doesn't mean you want violence, it just means you're looking for that sensation spike in order to get to orgasm. However, it also means we end up feeling guilty and alienated in ways that can then become a threat to our relationships.

It is absolutely possible to retrain our pleasure pathways. You can explore new types of intensity, new intentional storylines that can come from tenderness or slowness, but it takes time and conscious effort.

So what is the way forward?

The first step is to name what happened – that your orgasm did not come from the humiliation itself but from how that humiliation activated your nervous system. Only when you can recognise how your current arousal map was drawn can you begin to redraw it.

An extremely effective technique is to explore some sub-dom dynamics in non-abusive ways. You do not have to replicate the humiliation or pain; instead, try exploring verbal scripts where your partner uses authority in ways that feel playful and safe. For example, set consensual rules on what is acceptable for both of you without triggering you and then create scenes where your partner can play out authority roles, finishing with a long session of loving aftercare (see Chapter 54 for role plays and instructions on engaging in power play safely and respectfully, without falling into abusive patterns).

Next, we look at how the body reacts to memory. While masturbating, instead of returning to the old fantasies, try new stories that centre on emotional safety even if the sensations are far slower to build.

Simultaneously, change the environment, from the mental space of abuse physically go to weighted blankets, music, scent. These help ground the body and teach it to associate softness with stimulation. Remember this is not about reaching orgasm immediately, it's about teaching the nervous system that you can 'feel' in safety as well.

And finally try some sensory mapping during your intimate times. What parts of your body respond to touch when there is no pressure to climax? What happens when you focus on breath or subtle changes in pressure? Explain to your partner that your desire is for intensity, not abuse, so that he too can feel safe stepping out of his comfort zone a little.

The most meaningful progress will come from what you can reimagine together.

I don't think I've ever had an orgasm. What does it feel like? How will I know if I have one?

An orgasm is the intense, pulsing release of pleasure that happens at the peak of sexual excitement. It's when your body takes over – muscles tighten and release in waves, breath quickens, sensations rush, ending with a deep sense of relief, connection or calm.

Depending on what works for you, orgasms can be generated from almost any part of the body – the sexual organs or even parts of the body that one may not associate with sexual pleasure at all. There are mental climaxes driven by fantasy, and even energy orgasms, which involve building arousal through breath, focus and movement.

There is no fixed pattern to orgasms. Not only does everyone feel them differently but it can be different each time you have one.

Orgasms are triggered by the vagus nerve, which runs from the brain to the gut and branches through key organs along the way.

An orgasm happens when two parts of your nervous system – the one that builds excitement and the one that helps you relax – suddenly activate together. That clash creates an intense surge in the body, and depending on your physical and emotional state, it can show up as anything from feeling happy to crying, laughing, trembling uncontrollably, feeling nauseous or even just dissociating completely.

For some people orgasms show up as pain, often in unexpected and unrelated parts of the body, like migraines, leg or foot pain, abdominal cramping or tightness in the chest. Although it can be very distressing and off-putting, it is not necessarily a sign that something is wrong. However, if the pain is persistent, you should see a doctor to rule out any underlying issues.

Some people get 'dry orgasm', where the muscular contractions occur but without ejaculation. Some orgasm multiple times in quick succession, while others may take time to rebuild arousal again after one. Some orgasms are sharp and short, others unfold slowly, like a wave, and some are so mellow that they are missed altogether. Contrary to the loud, head-flinging 'yes, yes, yes' of films, in reality, an orgasm may sometimes feel like a soft ripple, a deep sigh or just a single contraction and nothing more. None of it is abnormal, it's just how your nervous system reacts.

It is extremely common (and normal) for people to orgasm through masturbation but not during partnered sex (see Chapter 18). Masturbation allows for consistent pressure, exact rhythm and zero performance anxiety – conditions that are often difficult to replicate during sex. Good chemistry is a must for good sex, but being 'excited enough' or 'in love enough' are not always the conditions your body needs for climax.

Vaginal orgasms during penetration are extremely uncommon, not because of lack of arousal or desire but simply because of anatomy. The majority of nerve endings in the female sexual organs are concentrated around the clitoris, far fewer deep inside the vagina, so unless you are also stimulating the clitoris through position, pressure or touch, orgasm is unlikely. Again, this is not a dysfunction, it's just how most female bodies are built.

If penetration alone does not lead to climax, there are countless other ways to bring a woman to orgasm. The *Kama Sutra* advises that a woman should be brought to pleasure at least twice *before* penetration, not just for her pleasure but to ease the pressure on both partners.

The intensity of an orgasm can also vary from day to day. For instance, around ovulation, orgasms often feel stronger and easier to reach as opposed to right before or during menstruation, which can be duller or more difficult.

Stress, anxiety, guilt, different kinds of stimulation (clitoral versus G-spot, fast versus slow, internal versus external), fatigue, dehydration, what you ate, all will impact your orgasm.

Even the stimulation you use works better on some days than others because of something as simple as your mood.

Orgasms change with age, but not in a bad way – just in a way that reflects the natural shifts in your body.

In your twenties, they are often quick and intense, but by your forties and fifties, hormonal shifts, especially during perimenopause and andropause, can make arousal slower to build. Muscle spasms may be fewer or less intense, and recovery time may increase, particularly for those with penises. It may take more time or different kinds of touch to feel fully aroused. Some areas, like the clitoris or penis tip, may become less sensitive, while other parts like nipples and inner thighs more so. Don't panic. These changes are not signs of decline but of sexual maturity. The key is to recognise that your body now needs different kinds of stimulation. Understand what feels good and work towards changing your approach to pleasure.

In most cases, decreased intensity is not inevitable; it is rather the result of accumulated lifestyle factors like inactivity, unmanaged stress and poor circulation, all of which can be resolved and reversed.

One common concern is that orgasms with a problematic or 'forbidden' partner can feel more intense than with a safe, loving one. This often happens because intensity – whether from fear, taboo or emotional chaos – drives sensation, and it is that intensity that pushes the body towards orgasm. Even when the situation is problematic, like conflict or abuse, the nervous system may convert that heightened state into physical release, not because it is good, but because it is intense, and that can make the experience feel more urgent or raw (see Chapter 49). Intensity does not always equal satisfaction, it just reflects how our brain is wired for automatic reaction.

In recent years, media and pop culture have turned orgasms into a kind of sexual milestone to be 'achieved'. From articles claiming women are not having enough to films showing explosive, perfectly timed climaxes, orgasm has gone from 'pleasure' to a performance goal.

Orgasms are a wonderful part of human sexuality, they can help release stress, boost happiness and build stronger, more intimate bonds between partners. But they're not the *only* part and they don't define the value of your sexual experiences. It's totally OK to enjoy sex without always 'getting there' and to focus on connection and pleasure in whatever way feels right for you.

Could you please talk about sex in the 50s for women who have menopause. What should they expect if they have sex after a long time?

We are told that sex is like riding a bike, you never forget how. Perhaps one doesn't 'forget', but no one prepares you for the levels of anxiety, discomfort and insecurity that come with retuning to it post-menopause, when your body, hormones and expectations have all shifted.

Let's talk about a few things we should all know, and how to move forward. The most documented impact on our sex life comes from estrogen levels dropping, which affects nearly every part of a woman's sexual anatomy. It causes the vaginal walls to become thinner, drier and less elastic, making penetration extremely uncomfortable. The blood flow to the genitals decreases, dulling sensitivity in the clitoris and vaginal entrance, so it can take longer to feel aroused. There is a higher risk of UTIs due to changes in vaginal pH. Even breasts may become less responsive in sensation quality. And on top of all this are the mood shifts, anxiety and poor sleep that can further reduce desire.

But it doesn't stop there. What is rarely discussed is that women also lose testosterone, often by up to 50 per cent by the time they reach their 50s, which not only decreases physical arousal but also the ability to feel mentally connected to desire. Nature really sets you up to feel 'flat' and unmotivated, but none of it is irreversible. Well-planned HRT can help restore many of the physical elements of desire – moisture, sensitivity and even the energy.

But the more important thing is to consciously understand that arousal is going to 'feel' different as well – slower, less spontaneous, more emotionally driven. It's not 'wrong', it's different. And instead of measuring new experiences against old ones, it's time to work with our body as it is now. Dry, tight and uncomfortable.

Post-menopause penetration can feel painful, not because you are 'tight' in the old sense, but because the fall in estrogen has made you drier and less elastic down there, and this discomfort can quickly turn into anticipatory anxiety, making the body tense up even more.

How to: Do not jump straight to penetration. Ask your doctor for vaginal estrogen, which will restore the moisture and elasticity to the vaginal walls. Use generous amounts of lubrication to make it smoother and avoid micro-tears. Practise self-touch or use dilators to gently reintroduce movement and sensation.

Rethinking pleasure

The stereotype of 'foreplay–intercourse–orgasm' is a bad template for pleasure at any time but post-menopause it is even more unrealistic. Not only do our bodies now need several alternative forms of intimacy to come to arousal because many of the old techniques and shortcuts no longer work but orgasms can be elusive as well. Your focus now needs to be pleasure. It's not about where it ends, but whether you feel good along the way. Because that will bring you back to it more willingly next time.

How to: Explore different forms of closeness (breast play, oral sex, sensual massage, etc.) and focus fully on the sensations and how they feel in your body – what feels good, what feels too much, what feels new.

Arousal may take longer

Post-menopause the brain takes longer to switch on, the blood flow to the genitals is slower and orgasms do not feel as intense – it's just how the body evolves over time.

How to: Think of arousal as a slow climb rather than a switch. Set aside more time for sex so you're not putting yourself under pressure to get there quicker. And focus on fantasy rather than just physical sensations to get you there.

Add erotic literature or podcasts to help rebuild the desire for desire.

Desire killers

Nothing kills libido like an overburdened brain. Chronic fatigue, work pressure, ageing parents and body image stress don't just reduce desire, they create resentment so that sometimes even the idea of sex feels like an attack. And once that cycle begins, it becomes harder and harder to imagine ever wanting it again.

How to: Create headspace for desire outside the bedroom – dancing, gardening, watching comedy, sensual rituals. Give your brain more than one reason to feel alive. Desire needs space to grow.

As someone who has gone through it, I can tell you that while the idea of sex after menopause can feel daunting, sometimes even impossible, it can also become more satisfying and fulfilling than it ever was before. In long-term relationships, sex often slips into a boring repetitive routine, and though we all know that effort and imagination help, most of us treat them as optional extras because they feel like hard work. But post-menopause, when your body no longer responds the way it used to, you are forced to change how you approach pleasure. And because we *expect* it to be difficult, we have a deeper appreciation of the pleasure we feel.

Most importantly, you begin to pay closer attention to what your body actually wants. Many of us grew up believing that discomfort or pain was a normal part of sex. But now, with menopause bringing real physical changes we actually speak about the pain, which in turn means you speak about how to adjust and pause in order to avoid it rather than push through it.

A colorectal surgeon's advice on anal sex

Dr Vani Vijay, Colorectal and Hernia Surgeon:
One of the most common fears around anal sex is pain, and understanding why it happens helps prevent it. The anal canal is controlled by two circular muscles – the external and internal sphincters. The external sphincter is voluntary, meaning you can consciously tighten or relax it. The internal sphincter, however, is involuntary and controlled by the brain. For example, when the rectum fills, the brain signals the internal sphincter to relax, but the external one stays shut until you are ready.

With anal penetration, the process is reversed. The outer sphincter must first be relaxed carefully, a step that many people either skip or don't do properly because they don't know how. As a result, penetration often happens before the body is ready, and since the area is dense with nerve endings and highly sensitive, any forceful entry can cause micro-tears and sharp pain. But when the outer muscle is eased open with care, the inner sphincter senses safety and begins to relax on its own, significantly reducing discomfort.

The cardinal rule for anal sex is consent–time–lube. Never, ever push in without warning, it is not a clever 'surprise', it is the worst approach to any kind of penetration, especially anal. The person must know what is about to happen so that the brain can prepare the body for it. In fact, pleasure practitioners will tell you that the slow build-up and shared control is a huge part of the arousal. It's not just about avoiding pain, this is what creates the right kind of intensity.

This means that time is crucial too. You cannot rush anal penetration, going in or pulling out because pulling out too quickly can also cause the muscles to clamp down and create sharp pain. For anal dilation, doctors will count to 10 while inserting, hold for 10 and count 10 while withdrawing because both sphincters work differently and both need time to adjust. Practitioners add that you need more time than that to prep for arousal and that penetration should always happen on the exhale, when the body is most relaxed.

The anal canal does not self-lubricate, so lube is absolutely essential and the application of the lube is an art in itself. The sphincters react to pressure, so if you insert anything too quickly or at the wrong angle, the body tightens instead of relaxing. Using generous amounts of lube, begin by gently massaging around the rim in circular motions with slow strokes. This helps the body register safety, reduces reflex tightening and allows the nerve endings to slowly awaken in order to build sensation for comfort and pleasure.

Finding the right lube can be tricky. Most commercial lubes are tested for vaginal use, not anal, so we don't know what kind of irritation or allergies they may cause on the sensitive anal tissue. Doctors use medicated lubricants containing lignocaine, which is not ideal for those practising anal sex for pleasure – numbing the area can reduce sensitivity and increase the risk of injury. Equally, coconut or castor oil are great for their soothing properties, but they are not condom-safe. Your best bet are high-quality, water-based or silicone-based lubes specifically labelled for anal use. Always do a patch test first to check for any irritation.

Some positions work better than others. For anal examinations patients are asked to lie on their left side because this puts the anal canal and rectum in a straight line, making insertion easier and more controlled. For pleasure practitioners the aim is the same – to get the back passage in as straight a line as possible – but there is more flexibility with the positions.

Side-lying (spooning), lying face-down with a pillow under the hips or being on all fours with the chest lowered will help straighten the rectal canal, while lowering the upper body helps relax the anal muscles and reduces pressure on the lower back.

Aftercare is essential. The anal tissue is delicate and needs time to recover, even if penetration was gentle. Coconut oil, pure aloe vera gel or petroleum jelly can help soothe irritation. Warm sitz baths (a shallow warm water tub) is great for relaxing the muscles and increase blood flow to the area to promote faster recovery.

Medically speaking, anal sex is not risk-free. The anal canal is not naturally designed for penetration, the lack of natural lubrication makes it high risk for micro-tears, fissures, incontinence, trauma and STDs. And so it needs immense care.

Enthusiasts agree that the right techniques and preparation are essential for ensuring pleasure and relative safety. Most problems occur when people rush or ignore pain signals. There is no such thing as an anal quickie, this needs to be treated as a slow ritual. The area is dense with nerve endings, which can produce incredible sensations and powerful orgasms. The act does not need to be demonised, just understood and approached with respect for the body's limits.

If you are dealing with haemorrhoids, fissures or inflammatory bowel conditions like Crohn's or colitis, it is essential to allow full healing – usually a minimum of six weeks – before attempting anal sex. In cases of proctitis, penetration should be completely avoided until the condition is fully resolved. Excessive or forceful stretching can lead to long-term issues like incontinence, especially as pelvic floor muscles naturally weaken with age.

Unlike the vagina, the anal canal does not have the same muscular elasticity and repeated pressure, particularly without proper technique, can reduce its tone over time.

Another common concern with anal sex is the danger of pooping. More often, the sensation is of wanting to poop rather than actually pooping because these nerves and pressure points are used to interpreting any fullness in the rectal area as 'I need to go'. This is particularly true for beginners, whose bodies have not learned to distinguish between the sensations of pleasure and urgency. If you have passed motion beforehand, your rectum should be empty, but sometimes there can be residual matter. So, while it can happen, it is not the norm.

Understand your body's routines, poop a couple of hours before to give your body time to fully evacuate and settle and avoid heavy meals or caffeine right before. However, if you still feel pressure, cramping or urgency, it is not the right time. A clean-out cannot override your body's real signals. Enemas or over-douching can hurt the rectal lining.

Sensations and safe practices during anal play

This section explores the sensations experienced during anal play because understanding physical responses can help promote safer, more pleasurable experiences. The aim is to fill in gaps in sex education and encourage informed consent and safe technique.

Pleasurable anal sex depends on the coordination of two powerful muscles that function in completely different ways – one is voluntary and responds to conscious control, while the other is involuntary and governed by the brain. Getting them to work in sync, at the right time and in the right way, is not easy and requires careful understanding and practice.

Important – each stage of penetration must happen on the exhale.

The very first sensations often come from rimming, which is a gentle stimulation of the anus using fingers, lips, or tongue in slow, massaging motions around the entrance. These first sensations are typically a mix of ticklishness and tightness because the body involuntarily clenches if the person is tense or nervous. However, as you continue the slow, consistent strokes, the external sphincter begins to recognise that there is no threat and will begin to relax. The relaxation at this point feels like a slight softening or a pulsing open–close reflex that gradually slows down. It becomes easier to breathe deeply and focus on the buildup.

Rimming is an essential part of anal foreplay in ensuring pleasure and comfort. But it can also be a complete experience on its own – different enough to add novelty, and pleasurable enough to build intense arousal without the need for penetration.

Once the outer rim relaxes, and you start to register pleasure not pain, you should feel a shift from nervousness to feeling more receptive. Take as long you need to reach this point, even if it means penetration doesn't happen that day. It may take a few sessions of foreplay before the body feels truly ready. The nerves around the anus are dense and highly responsive, so even external stimulation can feel intensely pleasurable, especially if it is rhythmic and not rushed. The pleasure at this point should feel like a warm wave, and breathing becomes easier. This is the state you need to reach because the experience of pleasure in anal sex depends heavily on relaxed, steady breathing.

As your partner begins to move inwards the body may again tense briefly. If you are fully relaxed and exhaling, the entry can feel like a slow stretch combined with pressure similar to the sensation before a bowel movement. If penetration is too fast or without sufficient lube, this can trigger sharp, burning pain but when the body is ready it can feel surprisingly satisfying, almost physically comforting.

Your next stop is the internal sphincter, an involuntary muscle that reacts more slowly than the outer one. Many people experience a second stage of tightness at this point. This muscle cannot be consciously relaxed, it responds only to safety signals from the brain, like steady breathing and the absence of pain or fear. It can take time to fully relax, especially if the body is tense or unprepared, and you cannot override it by simply pushing through. Forcing penetration too soon will clamp down the internal sphincter and often the outer muscle will clamp down too in response. But the patience is worth it because once this muscle relaxes, there is a noticeable shift – a sense of spaciousness, reduced resistance and significantly more pleasure.

Beyond the internal sphincter lies the prostate. Prostate stimulation is often described as one of the most intense forms of orgasm a man can experience. But because the prostate sits deep inside the body – around 5 to 7 cm in – it takes real patience and technique to reach it safely and enjoyably.

The first few times are best done with a finger as this gives you more control, it teaches you how to locate the prostate correctly and what angles and pressure you need.

Once past the internal sphincter, follow the front wall of the rectum – the side facing the belly button. Angle the finger slightly upward in a slow 'come here' motion. You are looking for a soft, spongy bulge, about the size of a walnut. If you move too quickly or use the wrong angle, it can be easy to miss.

If you feel

Pain – stop immediately.

Tensing up – pause and breathe.

Cramping or like you need to poop – pause, change angle or stop.

These are signs that the angle or pressure could be wrong or that the body is simply not ready.

What you want is a sense of fullness combined with a warm tingling and easy, deep breaths and relaxed body.

Once the prostate is located, use gentle, rhythmic pressure. The sensations will not feel like typical arousal at first. Many describe it as a slow, deep build-up of happiness. The orgasm, when it comes, can feel long-lasting and draining in a satisfying way.

Terms you should know

- *Rimming* involves oral stimulation of the anus using the finger, tongue and lips. Anal play should always start with rimming as it is an excellent way to gauge the readiness of the body.
- *Pegging* refers to anal penetration using a strap-on.
- *Prostate play* refers to the stimulation of the prostate during anal sex.
- *Butt plugs* are toys designed to be inserted and stay in place and have a very specific purpose outside of novelty

or visuals. While a butt plug does not move or thrust like other toys, it provides a constant sense of pressure and fullness. This steady sensation helps train the body to get used to the feeling of being filled without the added pressure of thrusting. It allows the sphincters to relax over time, teaches the body not to panic at the sensation of entry and prepares the muscles for deeper penetration. For beginners, using a small plug during foreplay or as part of a longer routine helps reduce the reflexive clenching that can happen with sudden penetration.

Anal training

Anal training involves gradually introducing the body to penetration. The goal is to teach the sphincters to relax on cue, understand your body's signals and the difference between discomfort and pain.

Bottoming refers to being the receiving partner in anal play. One of the more damaging myths is that bottoming is a sign of weakness because masculinity means 'always being in control'. In truth, being a sub does not mean being 'passive'. Bottoming allows you to lie back and let go of control, but it also demands a high level of self-knowledge for it to be truly pleasurable and safe – reading the body's signals, knowing when the breath tightens, when the muscles clench and when to pause. It takes strength to recognise your limits and assert them clearly.

You said in one of your podcasts that you can use BDSM to heal trauma and rebalance emotions. I always thought it was about pain and dominance and '50 Shades of Grey'. I am fascinated and would love to learn more.

Dana Shergill, Founder, Kinky Wellness:
BDSM is widely misunderstood as being about pain, punishment and power, and so heavily stigmatised that there is no constructive conversation around it, because even talking about it invites shame. Unfortunately, it is this same misconception that excites people and makes them want to try it and that is what makes it genuinely harmful – when something that needs extreme care and structure is practised without consent or understanding.

In reality, BDSM is one of the most emotionally aware forms of intimacy, built on negotiated control, careful communication and active consent. These qualities are what have made it an effective therapeutic tool as well. In controlled settings, kink is being used to help people understand the link between fantasy and sensation, and how the body and brain process those sensations. This can create opportunities to rebuild boundaries, work through emotions that threaten to overwhelm us and even work through trauma in a safe, contained way.

Let's break down the most common myths and see how we can use this as a tool.

Sub/Dom role play is one of the simplest and most powerful tools within BDSM because it allows you to communicate differently, because it puts you temporarily in a different identity so that you can express your wants, dislikes and boundaries without the shame or awkwardness that often surrounds such conversations in daily life. You don't need to stage huge filmy scenes. The whole role play can be entirely conversation, with both people just sitting side by side. Or if you're feeling adventurous you can experiment with standing/kneeling/lying down, etc.

The script too can be completely simple, where you tell someone what you want – simple sentences like 'do this to me like this' or 'tell me what you want' – while a sub may just do as they are directed. For instance, if you struggle to tell your partner that you do not enjoy something they do in bed because you do not want to hurt their feelings, or you have said it before and they did not listen, stepping into a dominant role can give you permission to take charge of their actions without guilt. In that role, giving direct instructions becomes part of the script, so you are not just 'criticising', you are playing out an agreed dynamic. On the other hand, if you are always under pressure to take charge, stepping into a submissive role can create a safe space to let go of that responsibility. In this role, asking to be told what to do, or requesting guidance, becomes part of the script. It is no longer seen as weakness or lack of initiative, but as an agreed way of playing. And because the roles and their boundaries are temporary and mutually agreed upon, they feel safe, not threatening.

Over time, these dynamics become emotional headspaces. When you need to let go of control, worry, overthinking, self-consciousness, etc. in order to access healthy vulnerability, you can go to your sub-space while the dom-space is there when you need to top up your confidence and authority without having to get aggressive. Whether you're wearing leathers and chains or normal jeans and a T-shirt, what you are really doing is using these roles as tools. Both roles offer structured ways to explore trust, emotion and personal growth within the safety of imaginative play.

Consensual non-consent (CNC) is possibly the most misunderstood of the BDSM practices. Contrary to popular misconception, this is not about danger or violence or about being violated, but rather a carefully structured, prenegotiated role play where partners agree to act out an intense dominance–resistance scenario underpinned by absolute trust and safety, with all boundaries in place. There is no unpredictability, every detail is discussed beforehand, every step is anticipated and a safe word is always in place so that the moment something feels overwhelming, everything stops.

For a lot of people, CNC is about intense pleasure because it allows access to extremely heightened sensations that would not typically be safe or desirable in real life. The (pretended) 'taking' or 'being taken' without 'obvious consent' creates a tension of resistance that plays with that edge, where fear flips into turn-on.

But CNC is also now being recognised as a tool for healing. For people who have experienced trauma, it offers a way to revisit sensations that once made them feel powerless or unsafe but this time with full knowledge of what is happening and the power to stop it at any time so that they can rewrite the experience. Each stage is planned and known, so you can confront triggers one at a time, on your own terms, in a setting where you feel protected so that you can control when to stop and how to handle the 'stop'.

Physically, this might include rehearsing the sensation of being pinned down, touched without warning or hearing specific words, and you include or exclude all these tasks as you wish. Each repetition builds safety, where there was once panic. Over time, the body learns that the sensation itself was not the problem, it was the context, the absence of choice.

Consensual non-consent is something people always find fascinating. This is not about violence, this is about enacting a role within a very safe space with someone who loves and cares for you and whose primary concern is your care and well-being. There are no dangers or unknown elements here; it is completely mutually agreed upon and done with knowing each step as it happens and a safe word in place for if it becomes too overwhelming. People often use this either to play out a fantasy in safety or to heal from trauma, where they can take charge of what happens at each point, which helps them take it closer and understand each sensation as it comes up so that each sensation can be dealt with one at a time.

Similarly, the pleasure in rough play comes not from violence but from the deliberate contrast between roughness and safety. In traditional BDSM each act, no matter how intense, is taught to end with a moment of tenderness – a gentle stroke, a kiss, a loving touch – so the body is not left in a state of continuous stress. It is not just one big release followed by one big round of aftercare. You go in and out of intensity in waves to heighten sensations and for the body to build trust in the experience.

Consent is the basis of each act. Before any play, you discuss what you want out of the experience – how each of you wants to feel mentally, emotionally and physically during and afterwards. What are your major turn-offs, small icks, distress triggers? What are your hard and soft boundaries – a hard boundary is non-negotiable, while soft boundaries may be open to exploration under specific circumstances.

Under careful supervision this is being used in therapy to develop emotional range without being overwhelmed or shutting down.

BDSM works best when approached with self-awareness and slow experimentation. Knowing your own limits before involving a partner makes the experience safer and more satisfying. Consent, safe words, pre-agreed signals on when to pause or stop and aftercare help build trust and restore emotional balance after intense play.

A practical guide to squirting

Half Moon Eyes, Adult performer, MakeLoveNotPorn:
Squirting is not quick or discreet.

It is not a type of 'orgasm', just a very intense reaction from the body that can happen with or without climax. The fluid comes from the Skene's glands and not the bladder. Having a semi-full bladder can help create the right amount of pressure – but it shouldn't make you uncomfortable. Many people prefer to pee 15–20 minutes before starting.

It is not something you force, and if you are rushed, stressed or over-focused on results, it will not happen.

Squirting is messy. It doesn't always gush out in huge amounts, it could just be a small trickle. But either way there is fluid and you need to prepare your space with that in mind. If you are not in the headspace to clean afterwards, don't choose that time to try it.

You will need about 45–60 minutes. This is not a quickie.

A bed, a firm mattress or even a yoga mat on the floor works. Make sure to put down several towels or a waterproof sheet.

Bathtubs are not ideal, they cannot fit the position your body needs to be lying down in and the cold, hard surface instinctively makes you clench.

Ensure privacy. If your brain is constantly worrying about interruptions, your body will not be able to 'let go'.

The first few attempts are usually easier in solo practice because you can take your time and focus on all the sensations you need without worrying about someone else's pace or expectations. If you do choose to try with a partner, make sure they understand this is just an exploration.

Mindset

Unlike masturbation that often starts with a mental fantasy or visuals to kick-start the brain, squirting requires the opposite. It builds up entirely from breath and the step-by-step progress of physical sensations.

This means no rushing to the 'good part' or clenching to pre-registered images.

You may still need to use fantasy to transition from real-life headspace to pleasure-headspace, but once there, you need to stay with what your body is feeling.

Begin with slow, non-goal-oriented stroking around the vulva and clitoris to resensitise your body. Breathe rhythmically into your belly.

You are not trying to get turned on. The aim here is to relax and unclench the pelvic floor and build up sensation so that the body can look for its own arousal.

Once you start to feel the body responding insert one or two fingers with lots of lube and begin stimulating the G-spot. The G-spot is located 1.5–2 inches inside the vaginal canal, on the front wall (towards the belly button).

Use a slow, steady 'come here' motion, applying pressure rather than speed – remember this is not about orgasming, you're building up. If it becomes too fast, you'll start to tighten the pelvic muscles in prep for orgasm.

Legs should be open and bent at the knees to keep the pelvic floor relaxed and unclenched. Do not squeeze them shut or arch too far. If you find you are clenching your thighs or curling your toes, consciously relax them. Tension in the legs often signals that the pelvic floor is closing, which blocks the release you are working towards.

At this point you may start to feel a growing pressure to pee – this is normal. The G-spot sits right behind the urethra, and stimulating it puts pressure on the bladder wall. It does not mean you actually need to pee, it's just the brain registering a familiar sensation. Do not clench or try to hold it in.

Instead, breathe deeply and keep stimulating gently. Your breathing plays a critical role here. Shallow breaths signal anxiety to the brain, while slow breathing says you're safe. The more predictable and soothing the rhythm, the easier it is for the body to let go.

If you keep going, that pressure should begin to shift. It may start to feel like a deep internal fullness, especially in the area just behind the pubic bone.

This is your cue that you are getting closer. If you can stay with the rhythm, it'll start to change into what feels like a tingling or warmth that radiates outwards to the belly, thighs or even down your legs.

At this point the arousal has built and so your body may try to go down another familiar pattern – the urge to clench your legs and hold your breath because this is where you would normally go for orgasm.

But if the aim is to squirt you need to consciously interrupt that instinct because if you can get past this it sets you on the path to the squirt.

At this point the sensations become so intense it feels almost unbearable – almost like a burning intensity in the pelvis or an intense shaking in the body or even an anxiety attack and the urge is to stop everything immediately.

The only thing to watch out for over here is pain. If there is no pain, stay with the intensity – let it crest, keep the body soft and breath steady. That is what allows the release to happen.

The squirting itself feels like a sudden drop in pressure and a rush of fluid. The fluid could be clear or slightly milky looking.

After squirting, you may feel shaky, sleepy or euphoric. Take time to rest and rehydrate. And as with sex, go for a pee – because as I've said before, the fluid here does not come from the bladder so that still needs to be emptied.

Clean up with a warm damp cloth and do not insert anything inside right away.

Ma'am I have weak erection and only last a few seconds. Am shy to go to the doc as my homies will get to know. How can I improve my time?

Dr Rena Malik, Urologist and Pelvic Surgeon:
Erectile dysfunction (ED) is one of the most common sexual concerns among men, but also one of the least honestly spoken about. Most men will experience it at some point in their lives, whether due to stress, illness, medication or age, but few are ever taught about the causes or treatment. And worse, in many communities, sexual performance is tied to masculinity and so ED is seen as a personal failure leading many men to hide the problem or try unregulated 'quick fixes' that worsen the situation.

ED can be broadly divided into two types – psychogenic and organic. Psychogenic ED is linked to stress, anxiety and performance pressure, which means that if the mind is anxious it can block the nervous system from sending blood to the penis, in turn blocking erections. Even if the problem originally started as a physical issue it can develop into a psychological barrier as well, because of the anxiety of repeated failures. This is why many men can continue to have strong morning erections or while watching porn but struggle to maintain an erection during partnered sex, because the performance pressure overrides the physical systems.

Organic ED is from physical causes like high blood pressure, cholesterol or diabetes. South Asian men are particularly vulnerable here, as these conditions are widespread in the community. Diabetes, for instance, triples the risk of ED.

In fact, ED is often an early warning sign of heart issues. Since the arteries supplying the penis are narrower than the heart arteries, a persistent loss of erection means that blood flow is being obstructed and this can be an early sign of a possible heart attack. Studies suggest that men with ED may experience a cardiac problem within five to seven years if underlying conditions are left untreated.

Things like prostate surgery and certain medications can also cause ED.

Low testosterone is another contributing factor, but much less than popularly believed. Only 3–6 per cent of ED cases are caused by testosterone deficiency alone. In most cases, it coexists with other underlying conditions and so hormone replacement without addressing lifestyle or psychological causes is unlikely to have much effect.

The first line of treatment for ED is not medication but lifestyle change. Regular exercise improves both blood flow and testosterone levels. Walking is excellent, or if that is not possible, even something as simple as 10 squats every 45 minutes can work wonders. These changes do not produce immediate results, but over time they address the underlying health issues that lead to ED. Without them, pills, injections or even surgery can only offer temporary relief.

When lifestyle changes alone are not enough, drugs like sildenafil (Viagra), tadalafil (Cialis), and vardenafil (Levitra) can help. It's important to note, however, that these drugs are not aphrodisiacs – they can improve blood flow to the penis but cannot create arousal on their own. Sexual stimulation is still required for the medication to be effective. Without mental or physical arousal, these medications will not trigger an erection. However, these medications do have side effects and should not be used in conjunction with nitrate medications, so speak to a doctor before starting.

A non-invasive drug-free alternative is the vacuum erection device, which works by creating suction to draw blood into the penis. Once the penis is engorged, a constriction ring is placed at the base to hold the blood in and maintain the erection long enough for intercourse. Since it does not rely on medication or hormonal changes it can be a useful alternative for people who need to avoid pharmaceutical solutions.

Kegel exercises are great, but they are not a fix for erectile dysfunction. They work by strengthening the muscles that compress the veins and help keep blood in the penis during an erection – but they do not address the root cause of most ED cases, which is poor blood circulation.

Many men assume that ED is simply a natural part of ageing, which often stops them from seeking help. While age does increase the likelihood of ED, it is not because the body is no longer capable of arousal, it is usually the result of lifestyle-related conditions such as diabetes, high cholesterol and hypertension, all of which affect blood flow which is the key to healthy erections. Men over 70 who remain physically active, eat well and manage stress can maintain well-functioning sexual lives. Perhaps if younger men were taught how directly their daily habits impact their erections in later life, we might see a healthier, better-informed next generation.

ED should never be treated only as a penile issue. It is a whole-person issue – physical, psychological, relational – and the most effective solutions are those that address all three levels together.

What next?

Erectile dysfunction is not the end of your sexual life but neither do you have to be in a relationship to seek help – your relationship with your own arousal matters too.

If you are experiencing ED, the first step is to rule out any underlying physical health issues. Book a check-up and test for diabetes, blood pressure and cholesterol levels. If you already have any of these conditions, work with your doctor to get them under control. Begin a simple but consistent physical routine, such as a 30-minute daily walk and strength exercises three times a week. These changes are not about 'curing' ED instantly but about creating a stronger foundation for long-term arousal and sexual health.

If anxiety or repeated failure is part of the problem, consider speaking to a therapist. Do not rely on social media advice or unregulated supplements. Most men with ED have a mixture of physical health issues combined with psychological barriers which needs to be carefully dealt with.

If oral medication is being used, make sure it is taken correctly. These drugs require sexual stimulation to work and must be planned in advance. Do not keep switching between brands or increasing dosage without medical advice. If pills fail, consult a urologist to discuss alternatives.

Does size matter?

My inbox is flooded with men asking how to increase their penis size, some worried about not being 'enough', some wondering if 'small' means 'infertile' but mostly just men wanting bragging rights from what they've picked up through porn or Reddit threads, the assumption behind all this being that size alone determines success in bed. So let's begin by saying that that is a complete myth.

While the global average for penis size is around 5 inches when erect, there is no universal 'ideal'. It is entirely dependent on individual preferences, what feels small to one person may be perfectly satisfying to another, and what seems large for someone else may not feel significant at all.

Physiologically, the nerve endings responsible for pleasure in the vagina are mostly concentrated in the first third of the vaginal canal and the clitoral network that surrounds its entrance. Going deeper is not what creates pleasure. What does make a difference is pace, pressure and muscle control – things that have nothing to do with size. And not so ironically, these are the very things that get neglected while the person fixates on length.

Interestingly, the *Kama Sutra* is built around the idea of mismatch. As Vatsyayana writes, no two people ever come together having first matched their genital size or sexual appetite – the idea is that no matter what the size, stamina or how much stimulation you require, one can overcome differences using positions, pace and pressure to create compatibility.

That said, there are people who enjoy the feeling of being 'filled up' – that sense of pressure and depth can be arousing. But even that's not purely about size – it can depend hugely on positions and angles of penetration.

For instance, putting a cushion under different parts of the body can change the angle of penetration to go really deep. Certain positions can also create far more sensation than deep penetration alone.

For instance, if the penis is smaller and the vagina wider the goal is to increase internal pressure and contact. The position 'Yugalaka', where the man enters from behind while both partners lie on their sides, thighs pressed together allows the woman to keep her legs partially closed, which tightens the vaginal canal around the penis and increases the sensation of pressure and friction for both partners.

The 'Tiryak', a variation of missionary, uses a cushion under her pelvis to tilt the vaginal canal upward, allowing deeper penetration even with a smaller penis. The elevation also helps with clitoral contact, especially if the man leans forward and uses his body weight to create more pressure.

For larger penises where the concern is around discomfort, the key is to avoid too deep penetration, especially in the beginning when arousal may still be building. 'Bhugna', another variation of the missionary, where the woman lies on her back with her feet on her partner's shoulders, allows her to control how deep or fast he can go and directs the pressure along the upper vaginal wall rather than through to the cervix directly.

The *Kama Sutra* doesn't give points for penis size, it gives instructions for creating pleasure through rhythm and responsiveness to create compatibility and that is what we should be focusing on, not this modern obsession with measurements. Because good sex is always about learning and adapting and negotiating.

Next, we look at pelvic floor muscle strength because this is where size truly becomes irrelevant. What creates sensation during sex is not just length or girth, but how well the body can move and respond. The pelvic floor muscles are what give you the ability to hold pressure and thrust with control. If they are weak, you may lose erection faster, and you and your partner may feel less, even if you are 'big'. The simplest way to train them is through Kegel exercises so you can learn to use them consciously during sex to grip or pulse.

Now let us talk about alternatives. I want you to remember that good sex is not about a 'prize' body part but rather the sensation you are trying to create. Ask your partner what kind of touch makes them feel most aroused. If they enjoy that 'filled-up' feeling, you can recreate it with your fingers, your tongue, or through mutual masturbation. If it only feels satisfying through traditional penetration, short thrusts at an angle and using your body weight to press down into them can make a noticeable difference to how size is experienced.

If the penis is thinner and you want to increase the sensation of fullness, you can insert one or two fingers alongside the penis during penetration. Place your fingers below your shaft and slide in gently using slow curved movements upward towards the front wall of the vagina. This will help increase the girth, stimulate sensitive areas, and build friction. Just make sure there is enough lubrication and your nails are clean and trimmed to avoid any injury.

The myth of the 'loose vagina' is as damaging as the size metric in men. Society has taught us that if either partner feels less sensation, the fault is with the woman's anatomy, in other words, the vagina is loose!

Vaginas do vary in size. While the vaginal canal itself is muscular and can stretch or contract as needed, body shape means some are naturally wider or narrower. But as we have said before, it is not size that creates pleasure, it is the ability to control and pulsate the muscles during arousal. So if the penis is smaller and the vagina is wider, understand what positions will help and strengthen that pelvic floor to enhance pleasure.

The biggest problem with mismatched genital sizes is that we don't talk enough about it. Whether you're hurting after sex but don't want to offend your partner, or whether you're underwhelmed and pretending to be satisfied, you just smile through it as though everything is fine. But all it does is lead to low-grade resentment.

And it doesn't have to be a dramatic sit-down talk about size, just small words – 'slower', 'not so deep', 'more pressure here' – will make all the difference.

Because yes, love does override size but not if one person is constantly adjusting and the other is pretending nothing needs to change – you have to meet halfway.

Bigger is not always better and smaller is not automatically a problem. Size alone has never been a guarantee of satisfaction. Technique and a genuine desire to pleasure your partner is.

PART 6

Conflict Resolution

Conflict is normal in relationships. There will always be differences between people. Most of us experience conflict with our partners, families and friends. Some of us are comfortable with conflict and address it, while others struggle and may avoid it or stay silent. In everyday conflict, we usually find ways to cope and resolve issues.

Researchers have broken communication styles into four types – aggressive, assertive, passive and passive-aggressive. In an ideal world if both parties can be assertive and express what they are feeling and thinking, conflicts can be negotiated and resolved. Unfortunately, it is rare that people are consistently assertive in a relationship. Depending on the time and phase of the conflict, the combinations can be numerous. For example, one partner may be aggressive while the other is passive-aggressive, or one may be assertive while the other is passive.

These combinations can become breeding grounds for relationship issues and conflict escalation. In systemic therapy, we call this 'the dance', where conflict in relationships is not linear, where one person is right and the other wrong, it is circular. It is about the push and pull. If one partner becomes aggressive and the other passive, you can imagine that this conflict will only worsen and eventually become a stalemate. These are the beginnings of long-lasting patterns within relationships. The work must involve both partners, not just one. If one partner reduces their aggression, the other must become more assertive and less passive. It is also important to mention that aggression does not always mean violence or anger – silence can also hold a lot of aggression.

While some may argue that our communication styles are fixed – for example, if a person is passive, then they are passive in all our relationships (romantic, familial or work), I wonder if this is entirely true. I believe people can behave differently in different contexts: in workspaces, with friends, within family dynamics and with partners. I also think communication styles can shift. We may act one way at one point of time but draw on different energy at another. Most importantly, I believe it depends on power dynamics, which also constantly shift within a relationship.

It is important to remember that conflict exists on a continuum. We have discussed everyday conflicts, which might sit on the lower end of the spectrum. On the other end, conflict can escalate into abuse and violence.

Here, I share a few elements related to sexual issues that might be present in a toxic relationship. To reiterate, this does not apply to situations where there is violence, and a person needs to leave to stay safe. Domestic and sexual violence are complex issues and need to be addressed with a lot of sensitivity and care.

Power and control

The need for power and control impacts most relationships. We are often so afraid of losing power or control that we may start engaging in behaviours that are toxic, manipulative, threatening or violent.

We need to ask ourselves: Why are we feeling the need to control? What do we fear? What will happen if we lose the power?

Often, the victim (the other partner) is unable to see these patterns clearly and interprets them as love, vulnerability or genuine need. For example, suicidal threats may not be seen as manipulative but as signs of dependency or deep love. Rather than creating boundaries and leaving a toxic relationship, the partner stays because they believe the other cannot live without them. A manipulative partner may pressure someone into activities they dislike, such as uncomfortable sexual acts, agreeing to a threesome or believing that infidelity happened due to their own shortcomings.

The manipulation can be so subtle and pervasive that we start believing the fault lies within us. We may become anxious or fearful that the partner will leave or cheat because of our 'limitations'. We may self-blame and feel inadequate.

These feelings create enormous stress. This is not healthy in any relationship. Compromise is essential in maintaining relationships. However, if one partner is compromising under pressure, or if only one person is doing all the compromising, the relationship will be impacted in the long run.

The key is communication. Each partner should have the space in the relationship to honestly express their feelings, needs, desires, comforts and discomforts. It is OK to talk about differences, and it is OK to disagree. Avoid labelling things as good or bad. Labelling prevents partners from being honest and open about their needs. It creates fear of judgement and closes off communication.

It is also important to remember that relationships are dynamic and work under circular causality. The blame game doesn't help. We need to understand relationship dynamics and patterns, that is, the dance. This understanding allows each partner to shift from their fixed positions and grow together.

Dr Anvita Madan-Bahel

My relationship has turned toxic, but each time I try to end it my partner threatens suicide – once he cut himself deliberately and left blood all over the bathroom. My friends said it was not real cuts, but how can I know for sure. I don't want anyone to get hurt, but I don't want to be in this relationship either. I feel even more guilty thinking he loves me so much that he would rather die than be without me whereas I am willing to walk away. I don't know what to do.

Threats of suicide in response to a breakup are not just emotionally distressing, they are a form of coercion. Whether the intention is manipulation or genuine desperation, the effect is the same – it forces the other person into a position of fear and guilt. And in that dynamic, you are not the villain, you are the one being emotionally controlled.

Unfortunately, popular media has romanticised these behaviours instead of condemning them. From Shakespeare's *Romeo and Juliet* to Bollywood characters like Kabir Singh or Kundan from *Raanjhanaa*, cinema is littered with stories of men who hurt themselves, or others, as a declaration of love. The subtext is always the same – that possessiveness and aggression equals intense love. And this isn't just bad storytelling, it's dangerous because it teaches us to read violence and emotional blackmail as deep and desirable passion.

Society has passed off emotional weaponisation as emotional vulnerability, and so when a partner threatens to hurt themselves 'if you end the relationship' it gets treated as a romantic climax instead of the serious red flag that it is. And the sad thing is that both people get stuck in this spiral, making it impossible for either to ask for help.

So whether it is said in anger, in tears or under the influence, it's important to remember that the intention of this statement is always the same – to trap you in a place where your desire for freedom or self-preservation feels like a threat to your partner's well-being.

Moreover, while all threats may not be genuine, all threats *are* serious. Whether it's a manipulative tactic or a cry for help, it needs to be handled by a professional. Partners are not trained mental health professionals, and it is no one's responsibility – or within their capacity – to become one overnight.

What next?

Let's start with the most important point – you are allowed to end this relationship.

You are allowed to change your mind, you are allowed to walk away, and you are allowed to prioritise your own needs and happiness without having to carry the weight of someone else's actions. This is not abandonment, this is survival.

When someone threatens to harm themselves if you leave, it's natural to feel frozen. You may feel that leaving makes you a bad person. But the truth is, staying in a relationship out of fear is not love, it's entrapment. And if you give in once, the cycle tends to repeat. The message becomes 'if you ever try to leave again, I'll hurt myself again' and that is emotional blackmail.

Unfortunately, threats of suicide often work, because most of us would not want to deliberately harm anyone, nor be the cause of that harm. And so it is essential that we lay out a clear road map of instructions that we can turn to, in case of need.

First, if your partner is threatening suicide, you will need someone else, possibly several people, to help both of you – a friend, a family member, a therapist, or even the police, depending on the severity of the threat. You are not a therapist so please don't try to counsel them yourself; this needs professional intervention. Hearing someone talk about self-harm, whether as manipulation or as a joke or a real threat, is extremely difficult and painful, and you should not have to navigate this on your own.

Next, draw a line. If the relationship has reached a point where your partner regularly threatens suicide each time you try to leave (or to get you to do something against your will), that's no longer a relationship, it is a form of emotional abuse based on your love for them or fear of what you think they might do. You are not helping them by staying, you're only prolonging a toxic cycle, because once you give in, the pattern will be repeated each time.

Importantly, don't try to leave during a volatile moment. People sometimes make these threats after drinking heavily – 'I'm drinking and I cannot be responsible for what I do next' or 'If you don't pick up the phone I will hurt myself'. Do not negotiate, make sure there is someone with you whom you can trust, and let a few close people know what's going on so you're not isolated.

Your safety comes first.

Some people, when confronted with the unacceptability of this threat, will say, 'I was only joking' or 'I was testing you'. You must let them know in no uncertain terms that you will not tolerate this kind of thing.

Hold your boundary. Do not negotiate under pressure. If you're leaving, be calm but firm. Avoid arguing or trying to 'prove' your reasons. Repeat your decision clearly and respectfully. Setting and maintaining boundaries is never easy. But if you can recognise that when someone threatens suicide to stop you from leaving, it is not romantic, it is a form of control, and just getting this clear for yourself can be a huge step in being able to make your decisions without letting emotions or fear cloud your judgement.

And finally, remind yourself, you are not responsible for their choices no matter how drastic.

Your partner's pain may be real, but it is not in your capacity to fix it, and you are not obligated to trade your mental health to protect theirs.

How can a woman who has experienced sexual abuse reconnect with her body, regain confidence in it, and feel secure in her sexuality and relationships?

Dr Anvita Madan-Bahel:
Sexual abuse leaves deep and lasting wounds not just on the body but on the mind and spirit. It destroys a person's sense of safety, messes up their relationship with their own body, and leaves them struggling with trust, intimacy, and self-worth. The trauma doesn't just impact one's sexual or intimate connections, it seeps into every aspect of life, from how you perceive yourself to how you engage with every other person in your life.

To answer your question, yes, healing is absolutely possible but it is not straightforward. The first instinct is often to wish that they could undo what has happened, to go back to life before the assault. But healing is not about going back; it's about reclaiming yourself from the demon that holds your mind captive. It's about being allowed to enjoy the present and future instead of being trapped in the perfect 'what was' and the terrible 'that happened'.

Many survivors respond by disconnecting entirely. The body no longer feels like home but like a site of danger. Even looking in the mirror or being touched, no matter how gently, can feel like a violation, and relationships suffer not because of lack of love but because vulnerability now seems threatening. And this is why healing is more than just moving on; it's about actively reclaiming what you need for your happiness.

What next?
First step – face the pain. Pretending it did not happen does not erase it; instead, it drives the trauma deeper into the body, where it begins to affect beliefs and behaviour in subtle, damaging ways. And by that I don't mean you have to 'relive'

the trauma but observe how it manifests in everyday life. Why does intimacy feel unsafe and touch threatening? Why does the idea of pleasure cause anxiety?

Please seriously consider working with a therapist. Therapy can provide a highly effective, non-judgemental space where you can unpack and understand the answers and access tools to begin reframing patterns and emotions.

The next step is to consciously work on rebuilding your relationship with your body. After abuse the body can start to feel like the enemy, you feel unsafe with the one person you have to live with permanently – yourself.

Finding the courage to practise body awareness is a scary step. The goal is to slowly develop a non-judgemental awareness of the body – not so that you can start to experience sensations but to understand that sensations happen.

Massage therapy can also be powerful. When touch becomes associated with harm, receiving safe, consensual touch in a controlled setting can help rewire that connection. Even self-massage, running your hands over your skin, can be a way to reintroduce comfort.

Small, empowering acts like wearing clothes that feel good, dancing in front of a mirror, or engaging in a physical activity that highlights the body's strength, whether it's swimming, running, or weightlifting, can help shift the perception from 'this body is a source of pain' to 'this body is mine, and it is strong'.

One of the most profound effects of sexual abuse is the disruption of personal boundaries. In complete contrast to what they are experiencing, survivors often struggle with saying 'no' and face real guilt for setting limits out of fear of rejection. Learning to set boundaries is not just about protecting oneself from harm; it is about affirming one's own needs and desires as valid.

This means recognising what feels safe and what doesn't, whether in friendships, relationships, or even casual social interactions. It means understanding that a boundary is not a rejection of others, but a form of self-respect. And it means having the confidence to enforce those boundaries without apology.

Trust is another major challenge. Past trauma teaches the mind to be hyper-vigilant, always scanning for danger, always expecting betrayal. Rebuilding trust, whether with a partner or within oneself, doesn't happen overnight. It requires patience, self-compassion, and the willingness to believe that not everyone will cause harm.

Then begins the journey of reclaiming your sexuality. For many survivors, sex is fraught with anxiety, confusion, and shame. The idea of pleasure feels foreign, and the expectation of intimacy can bring back feelings of fear and powerlessness. Reclaiming sexuality is about shifting the narrative from 'sex is something that happens to me' to 'sex is something I actively choose'.

This process does not have to involve a partner right away. It can begin with self-exploration, learning what feels good without pressure or expectation. This might mean rediscovering touch in a way that feels empowering, whether through mindful breathing, body appreciation, or even simply allowing oneself to acknowledge desire without judgement.

If and when you choose to re-enter a sexual relationship, open communication is key. A partner who is patient, understanding, and willing to move at your pace makes all the difference. Discussing needs, fears, and comfort levels before intimacy creates a sense of safety. There is no timeline, no rush to 'fix' anything. Healing is not about meeting someone else's expectations, it is about feeling ready on one's own terms.

Importantly, healing does not have to be a solitary journey. Connecting with others who have faced similar struggles can provide validation and encouragement. Support groups, survivor networks, and even trusted friends can offer perspectives that remind survivors they are not alone. The idea that strength comes from silence is a myth. True strength comes from acknowledging pain and choosing to heal in whatever way feels right. We each deserve to live without the weight of someone else's actions defining us. We deserve to feel safe in our own skin, to trust our own choices, and to embrace intimacy without fear.

Sexual trauma does not have to dictate anyone's future. The road to healing is not linear, and setbacks are part of the process, but every step towards reclaiming the body, rebuilding trust, and embracing sexuality is a victory. This journey is about more than recovery; it is about rediscovering joy, autonomy and the full, unburdened experience of being alive.

Non-consensual intimate videos

Let us be honest. Most leaks do not come from anonymous hackers. They come from someone you once loved and trusted, who assured you 'it's just for me' and then decided to use it against you. And the consequences, especially for women, can be devastating, and not just in terms of shame and social isolation but in terms of physical danger.

It's not a 'Gen Z evil'. Lovers have always exchanged messages, it's just that the medium has changed. It was love letters in my time, now it is photos and videos. And just as each one could be a treasured part of your love language, it could equally be weaponised and used against you.

Saying 'you cannot do it' never works – not only does it feel right in that moment but also you don't get into a relationship thinking that you may wake up one day to find that the very person you loved so much will one day want to blackmail you or want to destroy your reputation. Shaming or 'forbidding' just prompts people into doing it on the sly.

If you want to protect your loved ones, it is essential instead to educate them on safety and awareness measures.

Let's begin with the word 'consent' – consent is not an obstacle to be overcome, it is the ability to ask, listen to and respect your partner's wishes before you do anything that involves their bodies.

Recording someone when they have said no is not consent. Recording without telling them that you're doing it is not consent. Turning on the camera mid-act without discussion is not consent. Telling them after the fact and laughing it off as a joke is not consent. Assuming that it'll be fine since you're already having sex, that it's the same thing, is not consent, it is not the same thing. Recording them because they let you do it last time and thinking you don't need to ask again is not consent – consent is not a lifetime pass because it was given once, it needs to be ongoing and clear.

'You would do it if you loved me' is not consent.

'But you trust me, right?' is not consent.

'Everyone else does it, why are you being so dramatic?' is not consent.

'You are overthinking, it's just between us' is not consent.

'I'll delete it later, I promise' is not consent.

If you are not allowed to ask for it to be deleted at any time, it is not consent.

Coercing someone when they are drunk, high, emotionally vulnerable or trying to please you is not consent, it is exploitation.

Discuss boundaries in advance, how videos will be recorded, stored and whether they will be deleted if the relationship ends.

Unfortunately, however, the biggest obstacle sometimes is not that we don't understand what boundaries we need, it's the awkwardness around setting them. Women especially struggle with boundary-setting because we are not raised to stand our ground, we are raised to be 'agreeable'. And so pre-sex boundary-setting feels cold, unromantic, transactional – all the things we have been told will turn a man off.

If discussing terms feels too confrontational, turn it into a ritual. Create a 'consent contract' not in the formal sense but something symbolic. Curl up together and write a note on different things that each one likes or doesn't like in intimacy and add a section about videos including details like how the video will be recorded, where it will be stored, who will have access, and what will happen to it if the relationship ends. And then revisit it periodically because the more we experience the more we understand what we may want to add or subtract. This is not about mistrust, it is about digital hygiene.

And now for digital precautions. This may seem too tech but can be very useful.

As far as possible try to ensure that your face does not appear in the videos.

Record on your own device because any file saved on someone else's phone can be copied or shared without your knowledge. Never store intimate files in your main gallery or enable cloud backups.

Unfortunately, there are no foolproof systems in place to stop someone screen recording your intimate chat. Platforms like Signal, Telegram and Snapchat are recommended over WhatsApp or DMs but there is no way of guaranteeing safety because each one has a loophole that can be used to bypass systems.

If a video is leaked on a social media platform, your first step is not to panic but to document. Save all the messages, links, screenshots, etc. and report the content to the platform. Most platform websites have policies to remove non-consensual material.

There is also a service called StopNCII.org (Stop Non-Consensual Intimate Image abuse) that uses a technology called 'hashing' to create a digital fingerprint of your video, so if someone tries to upload the exact video on platforms like Facebook, Instagram, TikTok, it will recognise it and take it down. However, if the video has been altered in anyway (cropped, filtered or watermarked) or if it is on non-partnered sites or porn platforms, the system cannot catch it. Even so, this tool offers a first line of defence in a situation where most people feel powerless.

In India, non-consensual sharing of intimate content is illegal and a punishable offence. According to a lawyer friend, depending on the facts, you may file a case under Sections 66E, 67 and 67A of the Information Technology Act, 2000, which criminalises capturing, publishing and transmitting private, sexually explicit images or obscene content without consent. The Bharatiya Nyaya Sanhita 2023 supplements this with Section 77 on voyeurism and Section 294 on the distribution of obscene material, both punishable with imprisonment and fines as applicable. If you are afraid to go to the police, you can report to Cyber Crimes (cybercrime.gov.in) anonymously or access non-governmental organisations like SFLC.in and Internet Freedom Foundation or apps like Raksha and bSafe.

Again, no tool is completely foolproof, which is why boundaries are so important. It's about prevention rather than cure.

When your partner asks for an intimate video, even with your consent, I want you to ask yourself – if the video ever got leaked (for whatever reason) would you be able to handle the fallout without completely breaking down? If the answer is no, don't do it. Far too often it is the 'respectable' partner who thought it would be a funny or 'harmless' joke till it was too late.

The emotional toll of a leaked video is far worse than the leak itself. In small friend groups and university chats even a few shares can ruin reputations, leaving the person feeling they have no one to turn to and even more afraid of what the family will do to them.

If this ever happens to you, God forbid, I want to know you are not alone, and you WILL survive. Countless women have survived this; some have even fought back. Know that your life is not over. All you really need at this point is someone who will help you breathe.

The shame is not yours, it belongs entirely to the person who broke your trust.

I'm 31, he is 37, we have been married 2 years. Everything was fine between us until recently I found out he was exchanging nudes with a woman in Canada on Snapchat. I'm devastated.

On asking, initially he had no answers but last night he confessed that he did that because I was getting 'too spiritual' lately. (It was my daily routine – prayers, meditation, maala jaap, fasting on auspicious days, etc.)

And which is why he started getting less aroused and more respectful feelings towards me.

Also since we were planning on having a baby, we got ourselves tested and his sperm count was too low and he had issues staying erect, he said he was very ashamed of himself that he couldn't satisfy me and one day he came across this Snapchat thing and he started getting aroused and one fine day he got his feelings back for me and we had amazing sex. He said since his purpose was done he was going to delete the account but before that I saw it.

Do you think whatever he did is justified? Because to me this is cheating and I can never trust him again.

I would be grateful if you shared your perspective as it is draining me mentally.

Let's start by naming the cultural conditioning.

We have inherited a belief, not from our ancient texts but from later distortions, that sexuality and spirituality cannot coexist, that spirituality translates to a version of 'purity' that must mean an absence of all physical and sexual desire.

So being viewed as spiritual means you can no longer be seen as someone it is acceptable to desire sexually.

In a relationship this can become confusing. The partner who is practising the rituals may see them as simple, meaningful acts that should have no impact on intimacy, while the other steps back sexually out of respect. Both are left confused –

one wondering why they are no longer desirable, the other unsure how to approach intimacy without feeling they are violating an image of purity.

Because we have no model for how to communicate about this, it is a difficult issue to address. Simply asking a partner to be 'less spiritual' because it makes you uncomfortable is unthinkable because that would cast you as the 'bad one', the one 'corrupting' the other's purity. And because we have been socialised to treat conversations about sex as accusations rather than discussions, no matter how it is said, the reaction is rarely constructive. Since the partner practising spirituality is not viewed as doing anything 'wrong', your discomfort becomes the 'problem', and you are shamed as someone who 'can only think of sex'. Added to this, anything experimental or sensual is dismissed as 'Western' and 'not our culture', and desire is pushed outside the relationship, to be sought elsewhere in secret where there is no judgement.

This conditioning teaches men that lack of desire or physical issues are not problems to work through but rather almost to be expected. Instead of learning to communicate or seek medical help, the fallback becomes porn or 'cheating', because novelty offers excitement without effort or judgement.

It is not surprising that when he discovered he had erectile issues and low sperm count, he turned to Snapchat instead of speaking to you or seeing a doctor. And although it is extremely troubling, it is not unusual – men are taught to carry shame around performance and to avoid admitting to weakness, so many seek validation from outside sources where they believe they will not be judged.

What is truly problematic here is the gaslighting. Instead of taking responsibility for what he did, he has convinced you that your spirituality was the problem and that his cheating is what somehow fixed the problem, and that you should see this as a turning point where he is the hero and his betrayal the sacrifice made for the good of the relationship.

Now let's look at unclouded facts.

He consciously chose to exchange nudes with a stranger rather than deal with his own issues honestly. He did not tell you how he was feeling, he did not seek help and he did not take responsibility. Instead, he wants you to see his betrayal as the reason you both had 'amazing sex' again, which turns your pain almost into ingratitude.

First, you need to understand that absolutely none of this was your fault. You did not break trust, you did not step out of line, you did not violate any social contract. There was no harm caused, no threat posed, no behaviour that could be held up as inappropriate – nothing that justifies his actions and certainly nothing that shifts the blame onto you.

Next, whether you choose to stay or leave will ultimately be your decision because only you can decide how honest, deliberate or opportunistic he is being.

For instance, what is his behaviour now? Is he genuinely listening to what you have to say or is he still justifying his actions? Is he acknowledging the pain he caused, or minimising it? Is he taking responsibility for his behaviour or still shifting the blame?

And most important, how will trust be rebuilt? Will you find yourself constantly wondering if something is wrong even when it is not? At the first sign of distance will you be subconsciously bracing yourself for this 'fix' again – because according to him it worked last time.

And above all, what do you need from him now to feel safe again? What words, actions, plans do you need from him that will help you believe that trust can be restored?

These are not small questions, and they do not have easy answers.

For your own peace of mind, get professional support to deal with this because you cannot navigate this on your own, and overthinking will only drain you further.

I've only been in one relationship, but whenever I think of sex or masturbate, my ex comes into my head. How do I make this go away? I don't even love him any more.

Unlike porn, which provides a ready-made visual narrative, masturbation is not just a physical act – solo pleasure often depends on internal storytelling. And unlike partnered sex, where touch, sound, and interaction drive arousal, masturbation requires you to develop the entire experience in your mind.

That narrative might come from real memories, imagined scenarios, brief conversations, or moments that sparked something inside you. These images do not need to be romantic or even recent, they simply need to be erotically charged.

Your brain will naturally reach for the most familiar, vivid or accessible experiences to construct that narrative. So if your ex was your only sexual partner, it is entirely normal that memories of them come up during masturbation. Not because you want them back, but because that is the only reference your body and brain have for real, experienced pleasure.

In fact, from the number of people who write in with this exact question, I can say that most people, regardless of gender, fantasize about an ex at some point during solo sex. It is not because you want them back, but rather an arousal memory. You are not conjuring their personality or your past relationship – you are tapping into the moments your body remembers as pleasurable.

For instance, our stories tell us that when Kama, the god of love and desire, is destroyed by Shiva's third eye, his wife Rati rebuilds him through memory, crafting erotic visions, engaging in long periods of solitary erotic meditation, conjuring scenes of their past union, calling forth the sensations of his touch, scent and sound until, through sheer force of imagination, she reconstructs his erotic memory back into the world.

For me, this story mirrors how fantasy works – we don't just 'think' of people, we conjure sensations and desires through erotic images that the body and brain have archived.

Your ex was the only actual physical experience you've had, so him popping into your brain is entirely normal. If the sex was good, and if the breakup wasn't totally toxic, your brain will automatically use it as fuel. Those moments don't change just because the relationship ended.

Thinking about him while masturbating does not mean you desire him again. It's not even him particularly that you're thinking of, it's the excitement your brain remembers.

But now let's come to an alternative reality – what if you are in a relationship? Does fantasizing about an ex now mean something different? Is it a sign that you are not over them? Is it just a healthy fantasy or a warning about your current relationship?

Usually, no, but let's examine this anyway.

If you're worried, here are some questions that you can ask yourself to help understand your actions better. What gap is this fantasy filling? What benefit are you getting from these fantasies? What role is it playing in your life – is it just a tool for pleasure or a way to escape something you are not addressing?

It is natural to go through flat phases in long-term intimacy, and fantasy can be a useful tool to bring back novelty and excitement. But if you are using it as a crutch to endure the relationship or to make your present partner more 'bearable', that's a definite red flag.

That said, if you are feeling uncomfortable or frustrated by these recurring thoughts, there is always a way to shift them. Right now, it is drawing from a limited archive, but the brain is incredibly responsive to suggestion and the best way is not to resist the thought (because that usually just reinforces it) but to give your brain new material to work with.

What next?

Start by introducing new erotic material, stories, visuals, scenarios that feel exciting to you, even if they're purely fictional. Even if it initially feels like you're forcing something unnatural onto yourself, what you're really doing is giving yourself permission to imagine differently. At first, it may feel more like work than pleasure. But stick with it, because building new arousal pathways takes time.

And this is not just for this scenario – it is important to have variety in your mental arousal cues because your pleasure systems change regularly. One image or memory can only serve you for so long before it becomes dull or limiting. The more options your brain has, the easier it is to find something that matches the mood.

The next thing to do is disconnect the idea of fantasy from emotional connection. It is a common myth that thinking about your ex means you 'still have feelings for them'. It doesn't. Fantasy isn't a sign of longing; it is a shortcut to stimulation. Your ex is in the archives as 'something familiar' and that's all there is to it. And oddly enough, it's often the guilt about that thought which embeds it even deeper. Once you understand that, you can stop resisting the image and start redirecting it. If your mind starts there, let it, but then steer it somewhere else. It's not about erasing the memory but introducing other images that become stronger over time. And yes, even years later, an old image or the memory of a touch can resurface. But it doesn't mean you want that person again. It's just a memory of the 'sensation'.

Finally, shift your attention from what you're thinking to what you're feeling. Masturbation may be shaped by mental imagery, but we feel it in the body. Change your touch, try different positions, listen to guided self-pleasure audios –

anything that helps you stay anchored in sensation, rather than slipping into memory. Because once you start taking ownership of your pleasure, the stories in your head begin to change on their own.

The goal isn't to fear the images that wander into your mind. It is to build more of them, so you get to decide which ones stay.

I usually get very bad dreams which include sex as well and it becomes very horrifying at times.

When I discussed it with my mother the solution was to do some rituals and practices as they think I might be possessed.

Across time and cultures, people have been explaining sexual dreams as the work of spirits and demons that attack the unsuspecting at night.

In Christian folklore, the succubus, a female demon, was believed to seduce men and drain their life force, while the incubus (the male counterpart) targeted women and could impregnate them. Some accounts claimed they worked together, extracting semen from one victim and using it on another. These stories were often covers for sexual abuse within families, but communities responded with protective rituals – night prayers, salt under the bed or holy water sprinkled around the room.

In Arab folklore, the qarīnah (a female spirit) was said to have sex with people in their sleep with intentionally destructive consequences. Though invisible to most, some claimed to see her as a cat or dog and once again prayers, incense and amulets were used to ward her off.

In Buddhist scripture the Dharani Sutra promises those who pray that 'you will not be attacked by demons who either suck your energy or make love to you in your dreams'.

These stories have been used as a way to make sense of disturbing or taboo sexual experiences by casting them as supernatural attacks.

And although we now have scientific explanations for why these dreams happen, for many people the old superstitions still feel like the safest explanation. Especially when the dreams are violent or disturbing, it's easier to believe they must be a supernatural attack rather than accepting that the mind could generate something so graphic or 'shameful'. In those moments, when you can't find 'logic' the religious or spiritual remedies offer a sense of control.

The problem, however, starts when these experiences are buried under stigma. Ignoring the psychology or physiology behind the dreams, we instead label them as 'sinful' or signs of possession, we end up inducing guilt in the person, as though these dreams reflect some twisted deviancy within them, and this shame often causes more lasting damage than the dreams themselves. The spiritual practices are not the problem, it's that it can suppress the real problems that need dealing with.

For this chapter, I am drawing on the work of behavioural therapists and dream researchers who have studied sex dreams through the neurological and psychological lens to offer more nuanced and practical insights so you can try to understand what is happening with balance and clarity rather than superstition and fear.

Studies show that 8–10 per cent of adult dreams are sexual.

Dreams are where the brain tries to make sense of emotions it could not process during the day and they need to be understood symbolically, not literally. And since sex is one of the most emotionally intense experiences the body can access in a more regular and familiar way, sex dreams often become a symbol for unresolved conflict, power or vulnerability issues.

So if, for instance, you have had a particularly difficult or emotionally charged day – possibly involving conflict or stress – that has left you feeling powerless, the brain may translate this into an aggressive sex dream to work out the unresolved tensions. Rather than dreaming directly of the argument, the body registers the intensity while the mind disguises it through sexual imagery, especially if you struggle to express anger or fear openly.

Or if you dream about having sex with a stranger or even someone you actively dislike, it is often not about attraction at all but it possibly reflects situations in your life where you feel powerless or out of control. The content may be graphic, but the meaning often isn't.

The other fear for many people is that they also experience physical arousal during these dreams, in spite of how horrific or disturbing they are. Sex dreams occur most vividly during REM sleep, when brain activity is high and rational filters are off, which is why people may experience sensations of arousal even during unpleasant or confusing dreams.

We have discussed the phenomenon of arousal nonconcordance, which is that your body can respond to stimuli even when the mind feels distressed or disconnected – none of this reflects your character or your conscious desire.

What next?

The first and most important step is to separate shame from the experience. Sexual dreams, especially disturbing ones, are not a sign of moral 'badness' or possession. But in cultures where there is so much shame and silence around sex, we automatically learn that even the mind's subconscious nighttime activity has to be viewed with guilt. And to top it all, when elders respond with rituals or religious warnings instead of with empathy, it can deepen the fear that something is wrong with you.

There is nothing wrong with you, this is just how the body offloads tension. So instead of fear, treat the dreams as a signal that something inside needs your attention. Speak to a mental health professional to understand what your mind is trying to communicate.

Improving your sleep routine, such as avoiding screens at night or limiting food and caffeine close to bedtime, may also help.

Track your day to see what could have happened to trigger the dream, and work from that point.

Remember, the larger discomfort is coming not from the dream itself but from how we interpret it, that's what is making you believe you are morally suspect, or even dangerous.

So I want you to consciously remind yourself every time that generally this is just the brain doing its thing – filing away emotions and then exploring them in ways that help you to process the emotional charge.

Acknowledgements

It takes a village…

It may be my name on the cover but behind it stands an entire cast of co-conspirators who nudged, argued, encouraged, proofread, fact-checked, eye-rolled or simply reminded me to eat lunch – the biggest thank you to all of you.

To the fabulous and incomparable Anvita, who has so carefully shaped my skills as a sex educator, patiently poring over every question with me through the years as we unravelled the many tangled threads of human emotion and relationships – thank you.

To friends who patiently answered my endless, often weird, questions, sent me academic papers at 2 a.m. because I 'just needed to check one thing', cheerfully modelled pelvic floor exercises in public because 'it couldn't wait' and constantly reminded me that no idea is too strange until it has been tried at least twice – your love and laughter are woven into these pages – thank you.

To the anonymous question-askers online, this book is built on your curiosity. Without your honesty, these chapters would have remained sterile, textbook paragraphs instead of real conversations – thank you.

To those closest to me, who endured endless monologues about desire, guilt, purity, shame, sperm counts and the *Kama Sutra* while trapped on long car rides – your suffering has not been in vain.

To my team who kept my social media alive and my family who kept my body and soul together, as I drowned in the book – thank you.

A special thank you to Dr Allie, Dr Vijay, Dr Dasmahaptra, Dr Oishi Das, Nurse Theodore, Masooma Ranalvi, Dana

Shergill, Half Moon Eyes, Eric Chopra, Shan Boodram, Simar Puneet, Sonal Duggar, Kanishka Gupta, Smita Tharoor, Manav Chhabra, Zamiha Desai, my team Felicity Dukes, Garima Surana, Ameesha Raizada, Pranjal Mehdi, Arifa Raj, Sachin Rai, and my family Rahul, Nikki, Monica, Varun and Tarini.

And finally, to you, the reader. Every time you pick up a book like this, you join the invisible team that keeps these conversations alive. Thank you for your attention, your imagination and perhaps even your scepticism.

Resource List

Anvita Madan-Bahel
Psychosexual and Relational Therapist
www.cultureandtherapy.co.uk

Dr Rena Malik
Urologist and Pelvic Surgeon
https://renamalikmd.beehiiv.com/

Dr Pritha Dasmahapatra
Gynaecologist and Obstetrician
@tiptopped

Half Moon Eyes
Adult Content Creator
@Halfmooneyes

Dr Vani Vijay
Colorectal and Hernia Surgeon
@drvanivijay

Masooma Ranalvi
FGM Survivor and Co-Founder WeSpeakOut
www.wespeakout.org

Dana Shergill
BDSM coach
Founder, The Partition: Home of Kinky Wellness
Author of *Kinky Wellness Basics*
@kinky_wellness

Tanya Appachu
@yourinstalawyer

About the Author

Seema Anand is a storyteller, mythologist, sex educator and celebrated global authority on the erotic texts of ancient India. Bestselling author of *The Arts of Seduction* and anointed patron saint of pleasure, Anand is on a mission to show that when it comes to pleasure education, the past far outperforms the present.

Seema hoards books and handbags with equal devotion, convinced both can change a life, because knowledge and style are both equally powerful weapons.

You can reach her on seemaanand.net and @seemaanandstorytelling on Instagram.